JULIAN HAWTHORNE

Incredible Mysteries: Unsolved Disappearances Vol. 4

Contents

Denise Wells

In the heart of America's heartland, in Muskogee, Oklahoma, a new life began on September 22, 1970. Karen Denise Wells, the cherished daughter of Dorma and William Wells, entered the world on this fateful day. From her earliest moments, Denise, as she preferred to be called, exuded a sweetness and affection that made her the cherished beacon of her family's life. Her childhood in Haskell, a quaint town nestled in Muskogee County, was filled with the simple joys of small-town living, where the population danced around the 2,000 mark, fluctuating with the rhythm of rural life.

Growing up, Denise's curious nature and her caring heart were evident. She was a child who found joy in the ordinary, creating her own adventures in a town where entertainment options were limited but the natural beauty of Oklahoma's green landscapes offered endless possibilities for exploration.

But Denise's life was not without its challenges. As she navigated the tumultuous waters of adolescence, she found herself in the company of peers who, according to her concerned parents, might lead her astray. Despite their warnings, the fiery spirit of teenage resistance blazed in Denise, leading to inevitable clashes with her parents over her choices and friendships.

High school years at Haskell High saw Denise's academic focus waver, a common tale of a teenager more enamored with social life than studies. Her teachers saw potential unfulfilled, a bright mind captivated more by the allure of teenage friendships than the dry pages of textbooks.

Denise's journey took a turn when, seeking independence and perhaps escape from the constraints of her small-town life, she moved nearly a thousand miles away to South Dakota, living with an aunt in the historic city of Deadwood. This chapter of her life is shrouded in mystery, but it was marked by a brush with the law over check forgery, a misstep that saw her grappling with the consequences of her actions.

Returning to Oklahoma, Denise faced a new chapter of responsibility and hope: motherhood. Her son, William Blake, born in January 1993, became the center of her universe, a beacon of love and a catalyst for change. Denise's determination to provide for her child saw her taking various jobs, finally landing a role at Haskell Airport. It was here that her life took another twist, entwining with Michael Lee Douglas, the married man who ran the airport. Their affair, though fraught with the complexities of an unfulfilled promise and hidden love, marked a significant period in Denise's life.

April 1994 brought a call that would change everything. Melissa Shepherd, a high school friend now living a troubled life in North Bergen, New Jersey, reached out in despair. Denise, ever the loyal friend, immediately planned a rescue mission, a journey that would take her over 1,400 miles from Haskell to North Bergen, a daunting 21-hour drive.

The timeline of her trip is a patchwork of knowns and unknowns. She left Haskell on the evening of April 10th, in a rented Plymouth Acclaim, her own car left behind. Her route took her through Tulsa and towards Indianapolis, where she last contacted Melissa via a payphone.

The mystery deepens from here. What compelled Denise to embark on such a journey, to leave her son and life behind for a friend in need? Was it simply the call of friendship, or something more? Theories abound, but the truth remains elusive, lost in the mists of time and the vast expanse of the journey she undertook.

On the crisp morning of Tuesday, April 12th, at precisely 6:39 a.m., the unfolding mystery of Denise Wells' journey took a perplexing turn. Denise initiated a call to Melissa Shepard from Somerset, Pennsylvania, a location 450 miles east of Indianapolis where she was previously. This brief conversation was just a precursor to the baffling events that would soon follow.

Five hours later, at 11:39 a.m., Denise reached out to Melissa again. This time, the call was traced to Schaefer's Town, a quaint unincorporated community in Lebanon County. Intriguingly, Denise had covered only 180 miles from Somerset to Schaefer's Town in those five hours, a distance that typically requires less than three hours to traverse. This puzzling pace left many questions unanswered, especially considering she was now entering the final leg of her journey, with just 150 miles separating her from Melissa's home in North Bergen.

However, the timeline became increasingly convoluted as the day progressed. At 3:34 p.m., Denise made another call to Melissa, this time from Burnville, located 22 miles northeast of Schaefer's Town. Again, the pace of her travel raised eyebrows; why had it taken her five hours to cover a distance of less than 25 miles? Burnville was approximately 130 miles southwest of North Bergen, a distance she could have covered in the time it took her to get from Schaefer's Town to Burnville.

The situation grew even more mysterious by 5:27 p.m. Denise made yet another call to Melissa, but from an unexpected location - a Hess gas station along Route 11 in Middlesex Township. This call was a significant red flag in the timeline, as it indicated that Denise had inexplicably backtracked. Middlesex was approximately 72 miles west of Burnville, meaning Denise had been within two hours of her destination in North Bergen but had then turned around, driving back to Middlesex and increasing her remaining journey to nearly 200 miles. The rationale behind this sudden change in course remained a mystery, especially since Denise had previously called Melissa from Burnville, indicating her proximity to North Bergen.

At 5:45 p.m., Denise checked into the Pike Motel in Carlisle, a modest establishment just 1.2 miles from the Hess gas station where she last called. The motel, a simple brick building with external room access typical of budget accommodations, offered her a brief respite. Denise, appearing weary, expressed her desire to rent a room for just a few hours to rest. The motel owner, recognizing her exhaustion, kindly offered a discount.

In the following hour, four calls were made to Melissa from Denise's room. The contents of these calls remained undisclosed, shrouded in mystery. Approximately 15 to 20 minutes after checking in, Denise approached the front desk again, this time requesting a book of matches. This interaction likely occurred between 6:15 and 6:30 p.m., fitting within the timeline of the phone calls.

Around 30 minutes later, Melissa called the motel, inquiring about directions. The motel owner noted that after Denise's request for matches, she wasn't seen again. The last call from Denise's room to Melissa was placed at 8:05 p.m., where Denise mentioned she was lost, tired, and planning to visit a nearby McDonald's before returning to rest.

Melissa decided to drive to the motel herself, a decision that raised questions given the late hour and Denise's need for rest. Melissa arrived between 12:30 and 1:00 a.m. on Wednesday, only to find Denise's room unoccupied and her rental car missing. Noticing the room's disarray and the presence of Denise's key, Melissa alerted the Middlesex Township Police.

The police found no clear signs of struggle in the room. Denise's suitcases were intact, and a lit cigarette, which hadn't been smoked, sat in an ashtray, indicating a hasty departure. Melissa explained that she and Denise had been in constant communication during the trip, with Denise seemingly struggling with navigation.

The case, initially treated as a missing person investigation with no overt signs of foul play, took a dramatic turn with the discovery of Denise's abandoned rental car. At around 5:20 a.m., a driver reported the car deserted in the middle of Route 274, a remote and isolated stretch surrounded by the dense Tuscarora State Forest, 21 miles northwest of the Pike Motel.

The initial call to the authorities came from a frustrated driver who encountered the vehicle before sunrise. Navigating through the dense fog, he found Denise's car obstructing the road. Upon closer inspection, he discovered the car's battery was dead, an oddity compounded by the purse he found lying near the vehicle, which he placed inside the car.

Investigators arriving at the scene were greeted by the disarray inside the car. The interior was littered with fast-food wrappers and other refuse, indicating a journey sustained by quick meals on the go. Among the debris, wrappers from McDonald's and Hardee's were found, painting a picture of a harried and possibly disorganized trip.

The contents of the car raised more questions than answers. Denise's birth certificate, driver's license, and probation card were among the items discovered. Additionally, scattered items such as French fries, maps, shoes, and an empty soda bottle painted a chaotic scene. Complicating matters further were reports of two purses - one found by the motorist and a coin purse in a nearby ditch - though it remained unclear if they referred to the same item. The total amount of money recovered was a mere $13.71, further deepening the mystery.

Curiously absent were the keys to the rental car, which have never been found. The exterior condition of the vehicle suggested it had been driven roughly, with mud splatters and scratches hinting at an off-road excursion. The area around Route 274, known for its dirt and gravel side roads leading into the wilderness, presented a challenging landscape for investigators.

The discovery of the car, out of gas and abandoned in such an isolated location, added layers of complexity to the case. Was Denise lost or misled? Or was there another, more sinister reason for the car ending up there? These questions plagued investigators, who considered whether the car's location was a clue or a deliberate misdirection.

The intensive search that followed involved local authorities and Pennsylvania State Police, with tracking dogs and even helicopters scouring the rugged terrain of the Tuscarora State Forest. This search, however, yielded no significant leads or evidence directly linked to Denise.

As investigators delved into Denise's background and personal life, they found little to explain her disappearance beyond the check forgery charge. Friends and family staunchly denied any possibility of Denise being involved in drugs or leading a risky lifestyle, further muddying the waters of the investigation.

The perplexing backtrack of Denise's journey, her apparent difficulty in navigation, and the mysterious circumstances leading to the car's abandonment left authorities grasping for answers. Speculations abounded, but concrete evidence eluded them.

Family and friends, desperate for answers, converged on Pennsylvania, participating in searches and trying to piece together Denise's last known movements. Despite their efforts, the question of why Denise would end up in such a remote location remained unanswered.

The investigation expanded to include cooperation with authorities in Oklahoma, South Dakota, and New Jersey, but this broader scope failed to shed light on the situation. Theories were plentiful, but consistency and concrete evidence were sorely lacking.

Back in Oklahoma, Denise's father cared for her son, grappling with the uncharacteristic nature of her disappearance and the agonizing lack of communication. The family's confusion and distress were palpable, as each passing day brought more questions than answers.

As weeks turned into months, the case's complexity and the lack of substantial leads forced investigators to confront the possibility that the resolution might not be straightforward or imminent. Theories of abduction, murder, or a planned disappearance circulated, but without solid evidence, they remained speculative.

As the investigation into Denise Wells' disappearance continued, new information emerged, casting a shadow of complexity over the already baffling case. In the rental car, authorities found not only the previously known items but also a small amount of marijuana, a pipe, and a substance suspected to be cocaine. The presence of these items introduced new angles to consider, complicating the theories surrounding her disappearance.

Nearly six months after Denise vanished, her mother, De Orma, shared her heart-wrenching thoughts with the media. Her words reflected a deep sense of loss and a resigned acceptance of a grim reality. She expressed her belief that something tragic had occurred to Denise at the motel on that fateful night, a belief that was also shared by Corporal Less Freeling, the lead investigator on the case. Despite this shared belief, solid evidence to confirm a crime was still missing, leaving the case in a state of painful uncertainty.

Michael Douglas, the married man Denise had been involved with in Oklahoma, revealed his concerns about Denise's possible connection to drugs. He speculated that Denise might have been carrying drugs to Carlisle to help Melissa Shepard, a friend in a tight spot. This revelation aligned with the discovery of marijuana and the suspected cocaine in Denise's car, suggesting that drugs might have played a role in the events leading to her disappearance.

As 1994 drew to a close, the investigation remained stagnant, with no significant leads or suspects emerging. Back in Haskell, Denise's parents faced the heartache of celebrating the holidays with their grandson, a young boy now growing up without his mother's love.

The one-year anniversary of Denise's disappearance in April 1995 reignited the anguish and speculation. De Orma reiterated her belief that her daughter had fallen victim to a crime, possibly abducted from the motel or during her food run. Corporal Freeling, aligning with De Orma's views, expressed his own doubts about the rental car's involvement in the case. He suspected that Denise might not have been in the vehicle when it was abandoned and believed that someone in the area knew more than they were letting on.

Suspicion began to swirl around Melissa Shepard, Denise's friend. De Orma couldn't dismiss the possibility of Shepard's involvement, reflecting a growing distrust in those involved in the investigation, including the state police. However, Corporal Freeling clarified that while they were not satisfied with Shepard's answers, they did not consider her a suspect due to the lack of evidence of criminal activity.

Further complicating the case was the revelation of an unaccounted phone call made to Shepard's voicemail from a Sheetz convenience store in Middlesex, 17 hours before Denise was known to be in the area. This mysterious call suggested that someone else might be involved in Denise's disappearance.

The investigation uncovered inconsistencies in Shepard's statements and actions, including her arrival at the Pike Motel with two men, contrary to her initial claim of being accompanied by her boyfriend. These inconsistencies, coupled with her refusal to further cooperate with the investigation, deepened the mystery surrounding her involvement.

Additional details emerged that challenged the established timeline and narrative. A businessman claimed to have helped a woman matching Denise's description, who was asking for directions in the opposite direction of her supposed destination. This sighting, along with the discovery of an additional 700 unexplained miles on the rental car's odometer, raised further questions about Denise's movements and intentions.

In a perplexing twist, the wife of Michael Douglas reported receiving a phone call from someone claiming to be Denise, stating she was married and not returning home. This untraceable call, doubted by investigators, added another layer of intrigue to the already complex case.

The discovery of a phone call, made from a Sheetz convenience store in Middlesex to Melissa Shepard's voicemail, added a new layer of intrigue. This call, made 17 hours before Denise was known to be in the area, baffled investigators who couldn't rule out Denise or Melissa as the caller. This mysterious call pointed towards Byrne and Lebanon counties, areas Denise had traversed before inexplicably reversing her course toward the Pike Motel. Corporal Freeling, the investigator on the case, believed the case was solvable, but the crucial piece of evidence remained elusive.

Interest in the case peaked when a producer from the show "Unsolved Mysteries" visited Carlisle, considering featuring Denise's story. This attention was largely due to the persistent efforts of De Orma, Denise's mother, who had been tirelessly campaigning for more visibility for her daughter's case. However, despite initial interest and a thorough tour of key locations associated with the case, the show's executives ultimately decided not to proceed with the segment.

As time marched on, the case grew colder. By April 12, 1999, five years had passed since Denise was last seen, and despite a new investigator being assigned full-time, no significant leads had surfaced. By December 2002, Denise's case was one of the few unsolved murders in Cumberland County, Pennsylvania, since 1990. Denise remained a missing person, but investigators frequently included her in lists of unsolved homicides.

In November 2008, fourteen years after her disappearance, Middlesex Township detectives decided to revisit the case, hoping to leverage advancements in forensic technologies. Items found in Denise's car, like cigarette butts and paper cups, were prepped for additional DNA testing. However, even by April 2009, fifteen years later, investigators found themselves at a standstill. They had looked at persons of interest both locally and out of state but couldn't name anyone as a suspect.

David Freed, the Cumberland County District Attorney, revealed that they had been interviewing people who they believed knew more than they were saying. Ground-penetrating radar had been used around the Pike Motel without success, and there were indications of criminal activity in Denise's rental car, though specifics were not disclosed. The passage of time was seen as both a hindrance and a potential help, as statutes of limitations on smaller crimes might encourage those with information to come forward.

Fast forward to May 2018, 24 years after Denise vanished, and Trooper John Boardman took over the case. Boardman believed homicide was the most likely scenario but was puzzled by the lack of physical evidence and contradictions in key testimonies. He acknowledged potential missteps in the early stages of the investigation and the possibility that something close to the scene had been overlooked.

Boardman placed hope in new technologies, such as vacuum metal deposition, which could retrieve fingerprints from cloth. However, he was realistic about the case's prospects, knowing that it could remain unsolved for a long time unless a small but crucial piece of evidence emerged.

Karen Denise Wells, at the time of her disappearance, was a young woman with distinctive physical features, including a scar on her forearm and prescription eyeglasses. The last known location was the Pike Motel in Carlisle, Pennsylvania. Her rental car, a white 1993 Plymouth Acclaim, was found abandoned with additional mileage unaccounted for, traces of drugs, and no clear signs of a struggle. Denise's purse was found near the vehicle, but not inside.

The case of Karen Denise Wells remains a haunting enigma, a story of sudden disappearance, and a family's relentless search for answers. Despite the passage of time and the advancements in forensic technology, the mystery of what happened to Denise that fateful night continues to elude those who seek to uncover the truth.

Roberta Ferguson

Roberta Marie Ferguson's life story is a tapestry woven from diverse cultural threads, marked by personal triumphs and challenges. Born on November 19, 1968, in the heart of Canada's vast landscapes, Roberta entered the world as the youngest sibling in a bustling household of nine children. Her parents, Aaron E. and Mary Ferguson, instilled in their children a rich heritage, blending First Nations and European settler backgrounds, particularly from the Dunvegan Beaver Band. This cultural melange was a cornerstone of Roberta's identity, influencing her worldview and values.

The Fergusons resided in Grimshaw, a quaint town nestled in Northern Alberta, known for its close-knit community and serene surroundings. Here, Roberta's creativity blossomed. She found solace and expression in sketching and dancing, activities that allowed her to capture the beauty of her environment and heritage. A voracious reader with a penchant for humor, Roberta was both introspective and whimsical, often retreating into her own world of imagination and wit.

Mary Ferguson, a matriarch of strength and resilience, raised her children to be formidable and assertive. The family's darker complexion sometimes made them the target of racial prejudice, but Mary's guidance equipped her children with the fortitude to stand their ground against such adversity. This lesson in resilience was particularly poignant for Roberta, who shared a profound bond with her mother.

Tragedy struck when Roberta was just 14 years old. Her mother, Mary, succumbed to lupus, leaving a void in Roberta's life that was palpable and deep. This loss was compounded by Roberta's own health challenges; she was born with a congenital heart defect, a condition she managed with medication and resolve. The absence of her mother marked a turning point in Roberta's journey, reshaping her path in unforeseen ways.

In the ensuing years, Roberta's life was a nomadic journey of self-discovery and growth. She lived with her sisters Carol and Marilyn in Edmonton, finding solace and support in their company. Later, she spent summers with another sister in Surrey, a time marked by introspection and planning for the future. During these formative years, Roberta harbored aspirations of completing her high school education and dreamed of a life filled with love and partnership, often speaking of marriage with her boyfriend.

The summer of 1988 was a significant chapter in Roberta's life. In August, at the age of 19, she embarked on a camping trip to Sunnyside Campground at Cultus Lake in British Columbia. This trip, intended as a celebration with friends and family, including her niece, was to honor Roberta's completion of a work-study program. However, despite this achievement, Roberta found herself in a reflective, subdued state. Struggling with health issues and grappling with the emotional complexities of young adulthood, she faced this pivotal moment in her life with a mixture of apprehension and hope.

As the sun began to set on the tranquil surroundings of Cultus Lake, Roberta, overwhelmed by a longing for the familiar comfort of home, shared with her friends her intention to leave the campsite. Choosing to take the bus, she embarked on her journey home around 8 p.m., unknowingly leaving behind the last visual trace of her presence.

The morning after her departure, an unsettling silence loomed over the Ferguson family. Roberta, known for her considerate nature and consistent communication, had uncharacteristically fallen off the radar. Her absence sent ripples of anxiety through her family and friends, as it was entirely out of character for her not to inform her loved ones of her whereabouts or plans. This deviation from her usual behavior raised immediate alarm.

In their quest for answers, the Ferguson family approached the authorities, only to be met with a disheartening response. They were incorrectly informed that it was too early to file a missing-person report, a misconception that unfortunately delayed the investigation. In Canada, there is no mandated waiting period to report someone as missing, a fact that was overlooked in Roberta's case. This crucial misunderstanding resulted in lost time, time that could have been pivotal in uncovering her whereabouts.

Determined and desperate, the Ferguson family took matters into their own hands. They embarked on a grassroots campaign, printing and distributing missing person posters far and wide, and driving to Cultus Lake in a relentless search for Roberta. This display of familial tenacity and love was a testament to their unyielding hope of finding her.

The police eventually joined the search, but the delay in their involvement cast a shadow over the investigation. The initial hours and days following a disappearance are often critical in finding leads, and in Roberta's case, this window had tragically closed without any substantial progress.

The mystery of Roberta Ferguson's disappearance continued to loom large, with no concrete evidence or trace of her ever surfacing. Theories abounded, with some speculating that perhaps Roberta had chosen to start a new life elsewhere. However, this theory clashed with the reality of her life – her recent academic success, plans of a future with her partner, and her ongoing health challenges. These factors painted a picture of a young woman anchored to her present life, making the idea of her voluntarily starting anew seem unlikely.

Known to her loved ones as a person of good character, Roberta was not known to engage in activities involving alcohol or drugs. She steered clear of parties and had never previously run away from home, painting a portrait of a young woman grounded in stability and routine.

The theory of abduction by a stranger has often been considered in Roberta's case, yet it remains shrouded in uncertainty due to a lack of concrete evidence. This theory, along with several others, has been a source of endless speculation and concern for the Ferguson family, particularly regarding the circumstances leading up to her disappearance. One point of contention was the decision of Roberta's friends to allow her to journey alone to the bus station, especially given her ill health at the time. The expectation of basic decency would suggest that accompanying her to ensure her safety would have been the more responsible choice.

The possibility that Roberta may have hitchhiked to the station was also considered. However, it remains unclear whether she ever reached her intended destination. Shortly after her departure, a woman fitting Roberta's description was reportedly seen conversing with the driver of a red sports car at the intersection of Vedder Mountain Road and Cultus Lake Road. The driver, described as an average height man with blond or light brown hair and a prominent jawline, remains unidentified, adding yet another layer of mystery to the case.

Authorities have suspected foul play in Roberta's disappearance, leading them to explore connections with known criminals. One such individual was serial killer Robert Pickton, infamously known as the "Pig Farm Killer". Though Pickton's usual victims differed significantly from Roberta in profile, his heinous desire to reach a morbid tally of 50 kills brought him under scrutiny. However, DNA samples provided by the Ferguson family did not match any remains found on Pickton's farm.

Another person of interest was Terry Arnold, a convicted murderer who, at one point, claimed to be the last person to see the 19-year-old alive. His access to a red hatchback car around the time of Roberta's disappearance cast further suspicion. Following his death in 2005, a note was discovered in Arnold's handwriting, declaring his innocence in Roberta's disappearance and in the crimes for which he was convicted. The Ferguson family, however, remained convinced of Arnold's involvement, though the truth about his alleged confession may never be fully uncovered.

When Roberta vanished, she was described as being 5 feet 5 inches tall, weighing between 115 to 120 pounds, with long, curly dark brown or black hair, brown eyes, and typically wearing glasses. Her last known attire included octagon eyeglasses, a blue-black tank top, black stretchy trousers rolled up to her knees, white running shoes with dirt marks, and an army khaki green rucksack.

Roberta's case, along with thousands of others involving Indigenous women, has tragically not received the attention it deserves. According to a 2014 RCMP report, Roberta's case is one of 225 unsolved disappearances and murders of Indigenous women. Her sisters continue to advocate for more thorough investigations in such cases, highlighting a critical need for change in how these disappearances are handled.

Marshal Iwaasa

Born on January 3, 1993, in Lethbridge, Alberta, Canada, Marshal was the cherished son of Tammy Johnson and Perry Iwaasa. He shared his childhood with an older sister, Paige, who vividly recalls their formative years. Their father, Perry, had become a distant figure in their lives, having not been involved for a decade prior to Marshal's baffling disappearance. This familial backdrop painted a picture of a close-knit trio: Marshal, Tammy, and Paige, navigating life's complexities together.

Paige's recollections of Marshal are tender and detailed, portraying him as a gentle soul, quiet yet profoundly kind. His easy-going nature was exemplified in heartwarming anecdotes, such as the time he rescued an injured bird entangled in a fence, showcasing his calm and compassionate demeanor. Even when faced with personal setbacks, like his sister accidentally damaging his new truck, Marshal's reaction was one of understanding and forgiveness, rather than anger.

Marshal's childhood and teenage years were filled with a variety of interests. He was an active participant in sports like football and rugby but eventually stepped away from these activities, guided by a deep-seated aversion to causing harm to others. His love for the outdoors was unmistakable, with camping, hiking, and swimming being cherished activities. He and Paige shared a special bond over these outdoor adventures and memorable trips to places like Hawaii.

During his school years, Marshal was known to have a close-knit circle of friends, relationships he maintained throughout his life. Post high-school, Marshal's interests evolved towards fitness and bodybuilding, leading him to forge new friendships in these communities while staying connected with his high school companions. His early work life saw him in various roles, from a grocery store employee to physical labor jobs in the gas industry and powerline work.

A pivotal moment in Marshal's life came with his decision to pursue a career in technology. He enrolled in a software development program at the Southern Alberta University of Technology for the 2018-2019 academic year, prompting a move from Lethbridge to Calgary. During this period, Paige moved to Hawaii, and their communication, although less frequent due to Marshal's busy schedule, remained a constant in their lives.

However, things took a curious turn in the fall of 2019. Marshal, expected to re-enroll in his program, did not register for the semester. This revelation surfaced during a family reunion in the summer of 2019, where Marshal's vague responses about the importance of experience over formal education in his field raised questions about his future plans. His family, respecting his privacy, did not press further, trusting in his judgment.

In the two months leading up to his disappearance, Paige noticed a discernible change in Marshal's behavior. He became more elusive, often taking weeks to respond to her messages. This shift was perplexing but not entirely out of character for the introverted Marshal. The siblings also shared a storage unit, a repository of their shared memories and belongings, which played a role in the events leading up to Marshal's disappearance.

The fateful day of November 17, 2019, saw Marshal engage in ordinary activities like cleaning his apartment and doing laundry before his planned visit to his mother in Lethbridge. The visit was brief but normal, with Marshal assisting his mother with computer issues and showing no signs of distress.

He left late in the evening, intending to stop by the storage unit and return to Calgary, a plan that his mother, concerned about the late hour, gently objected to.

The storage unit visit was the last confirmed sighting of Marshal. What transpired afterwards remains shrouded in mystery, a puzzle that has left family, friends, and the community with more questions than answers.

On that fateful night, Marshal Iwaasa's efforts to access the storage unit he shared with his sister Paige unfolded like a scene from a suspenseful narrative. The logs from the facility tell a story of persistence and frustration: Marshal trying his code repeatedly, taking breaks, then resuming his attempts. This persistence was characteristic of Marshal, reflecting his determination to accomplish what he set out to do.

Paige recounts that they were unaware of a change in the storage unit's access policy. Initially, they had 24-hour access, but unbeknownst to them, this had been restricted to certain hours. This crucial piece of information came to light only when Marshal found himself unable to enter the facility that night. The security measures of the storage unit were such that each user had an individual code, linking access directly to the person. Since Paige and Marshal were the only ones privy to their code, it was clear that it was Marshal attempting to gain entry.

Despite his numerous unsuccessful attempts, Marshal's determination did not wane. He waited until 6 AM on Monday, November 18th, when the facility finally opened. He spent about an hour and a half inside the unit before leaving around 8:30 AM. This visit to the storage unit marks the last known whereabouts of Marshal Iwaasa. Tragically, by the time his family realized he was missing, the storage unit's security footage had already been erased, leaving a void of crucial information.

The mystery deepens with the question of why Marshal chose not to spend the night at his mother's house, which was a mere 15-minute drive away. If he was determined to access the storage unit at the earliest possible time, he could have easily stayed with his mother and returned early in the morning. Yet, he chose otherwise, and the reasons behind this decision remain a perplexing enigma.

In the following days, Paige's concern grew as she realized she hadn't heard from Marshal in a while. His phone was disconnected, a not uncommon occurrence for him, as he often let his phone run out of minutes. Paige tried reaching out via email, another usual mode of communication, but to no avail. Even his mother hadn't heard from him, and his friends were equally in the dark. This was uncharacteristic of Marshal, who, despite being introverted, would usually check in with someone.

The situation took a dramatic and concerning turn on November 22nd, 2019. While Tammy, Marshal's mother, was visiting Paige in Hawaii, they received a distressing call from the authorities. Marshal's truck, a dark blue 2009 GMC Sierra, was discovered by hikers at a trailhead in a rural area north of Pemberton, British Columbia, a staggering 12 to 16-hour drive from Lethbridge. The truck was found in a severely burnt state, almost unrecognizable.

The location of the discovery was particularly baffling. The truck was at the trailhead for Brian Waddington Hut, a remote area in dense forest, accessible only via rough terrain requiring a four-wheel drive. The absence of cell service in this area meant GPS navigation was impossible. From the trailhead, it was a two to three-hour hike to the hut, which required prior registration for overnight stays. The police checked the hut's logs and confirmed that not only had Marshal not registered for that night, but he had never visited this hut before. This raised serious questions about why his truck was found in such a secluded and specific location, especially given that Marshal had mentioned having trouble with his truck's four-wheel drive.

Adding to the mystery, various personal belongings were scattered around the burnt truck, including three smashed cell phones belonging to Marshal, clothing, an Xbox, a PlayStation, and his expired passport. Initially, it was thought that the gaming consoles were Marshal's, but a visit to his apartment by Paige revealed his own consoles were still there, suggesting these belonged to someone else. Missing from the scene were Marshal's backpack, laptop, contact lenses and solution, wallet, and current cell phone.

Among the items found scattered around the truck were several old, smashed cell phones. This was not entirely unusual for Marshal, as his family knew he often acquired used phones and was prone to breaking them. These phones, found in various states of disrepair, were a common sight in Marshal's possession, leading his family to pay more attention to the absence of his current phone, which was notably missing from the scene.

The discovery of the truck itself was a feat, given the lack of cell service in the area. The hikers who first stumbled upon the burnt vehicle had to hike back to a location with cell service to report their find. The Royal Canadian Mounted Police (RCMP) faced significant challenges in reaching the site. The difficulty of the terrain was so extreme that one of their vehicles sustained damage during the attempt.

Adding to the complexity, the original witnesses to the scene took photographs, which later proved crucial. When the RCMP finally reached the site, discrepancies were noted between these photographs and the state of the scene. For instance, the cell phones, initially scattered in the initial photos, were later found neatly placed next to each other. Additionally, the steering column of the truck had been removed, a detail that the RCMP confirmed they did not initiate. This raised questions about whether the items were tampered with by someone involved in the case or by curious passersby during the two days it took for the police to access the site.

The RCMP called for anyone in the area during those days to come forward with information, especially if they had unintentionally disturbed the scene. However, as far as public knowledge goes, no one has come forward with such information. The investigation was further hampered by the inability to move the truck from the site for a more thorough examination in a controlled environment. The rugged terrain made it impossible to tow the truck, and it remains in place to this day.

The investigation into Marshal's disappearance and the circumstances surrounding the discovery of his truck has been a source of frustration for his family. They have expressed dissatisfaction with the RCMP's handling of the investigation, particularly regarding the lack of testing on the numerous items recovered from the scene. The family's concerns revolve around the potential for undiscovered DNA or fingerprints on these items, which could provide crucial leads in the case.

In response, the RCMP has stated that DNA testing in their crime labs requires reasonable grounds to believe a DNA-designated criminal offense has been committed. As of now, they have not found sufficient evidence to justify such testing. While Marshal's disappearance is considered suspicious, the RCMP has not yet concluded that criminal activity is involved.

In their investigation, the RCMP has monitored Marshal's social media, bank accounts, and cell phone, finding no activity since November 15th. They have also reviewed surveillance footage along possible routes Marshal could have taken from Lethbridge to the location where his truck was found, but to no avail. Bank records were also scrutinized to track any purchases, particularly gas, that Marshal might have made during his journey, but this too yielded no results.

One of the most baffling aspects is how Marshal, with his distinctive tattoos and hair, could travel such a long distance without being recognized or captured on any surveillance footage, especially considering the need for gas refills during his extensive journey. The route from Lethbridge to Pemberton, where his truck was eventually found, is not only long but includes challenging terrains that demand a slow and careful drive. This raises the question: how did he manage to travel this distance without a trace, not even a single gas stop recorded or witnessed?

The RCMP's extensive search efforts, involving cadaver dogs, ATVs, and helicopters, yielded no tangible results. Additionally, their collaboration with a fire investigator indicated the use of an accelerant in the burning of Marshal's truck, yet further details remain scarce. The police have been notably reticent in sharing information, both with the public and Marshal's family, fostering a sense of frustration and helplessness among those desperate for answers.

This reticence from the authorities, while understandable in preserving the integrity of the investigation, has led to rampant speculation and the development of multiple theories. One such theory suggests the possibility of Marshal leaving of his own accord, prompted by stress and a sense of withdrawal from his usual life. His unexpected decision not to re-enroll in school, only discovered post-disappearance, adds weight to this theory. However, the specific choice of the remote location in British Columbia for the burning of his truck, and the lack of financial or digital traces, complicates this theory.

On the other hand, the theory of foul play cannot be dismissed. Lethbridge's reputation for crime and drug activity raises the possibility of Marshal unwittingly becoming entangled with dangerous individuals. His non-confrontational nature could have made him a vulnerable target in a potentially volatile situation, possibly leading to his harm and the subsequent burning of his truck to destroy evidence.

The discovery of Marshal's personal belongings scattered around his burnt truck, including his expired passport, adds another layer of mystery. Why were these items discarded in such a manner, and what led to the decision to burn the truck? If Marshal intended to start anew or hide, why draw attention with such a dramatic act?

Furthermore, the time Marshal spent at the storage unit before his disappearance is a crucial yet opaque part of the puzzle. It's unknown whether this visit was a mundane errand or a pivotal moment related to his disappearance. Was he meeting someone, hiding, or retrieving something significant?

As we delve into these theories, it's vital to consider all angles. Was Marshal's disappearance a deliberate act to start over, or was he a victim of an unforeseen and tragic circumstance? The lack of a clear motive, combined with the mysterious circumstances of the burning truck and the absence of digital footprints, leaves us oscillating between these possibilities.

In the end, the key to unraveling this enigma may lie in raising awareness of Marshal's case and encouraging those with potential information to come forward. The solution to this perplexing mystery might just be within reach, waiting for the right piece of information to shed light on the fate of Marshal Iwaasa.

Jennifer Pentilla

Born on March 4, 1973, in the picturesque landscapes of Montana, Jennifer was the cherished daughter of Nicholas and Lynn. Raised in an environment that nurtured her intelligence, kindness, and attentiveness, Jennifer quickly became known as a young woman with a heart set on helping others.

From a tender age of two, Jennifer's life was enriched with the arrival of her younger sister, Carrie. The bond between the sisters was one of deep affection and camaraderie, as they grew up sharing countless moments of joy and laughter. Jennifer, while always up for a good laugh, had a side to her that was profoundly serious, especially when it came to her spiritual life. A devout Lutheran, her faith was the cornerstone of her existence, guiding her through life's twists and turns.

Jennifer's grandmother fondly recalled to the Montana Standard how Jennifer steered clear of any vices. She was the epitome of a 'plain Jane girl'—a description that her mother agreed with but also added that Jennifer was far from ordinary. Once Jennifer set her mind to something, it was almost impossible to sway her. This trait was particularly evident in her adventurous spirit and her unquenchable thirst to explore and assist others globally.

During her junior year at Great Falls High School, Jennifer's curiosity about the world was piqued by the prospect of participating in an exchange program. Through the Open Door program, she seized the opportunity to spend four memorable weeks in Ivory Coast, West Africa, in the summer of 1990. While the trip did not entirely align with her expectations—she found herself in a luxurious home rather than the humble settings she had envisioned—it nevertheless was a transformative experience. Her mother, Lynn, recounted to the Great Falls Tribune how Jennifer longed to be closer to the people, aiding them directly.

This trip was a pivotal moment for Jennifer. It shaped her worldview and ignited a burning desire to do more. However, life was not without its trials. In October 1990, as she was stepping into her senior year, tragedy struck. Jennifer's father lost his battle with cancer, passing away at the young age of 44. This loss was a profound challenge for Jennifer, but she found solace in her unwavering faith. As her mother recounted, Jennifer believed it was part of a divine plan—that her father had a higher purpose to fulfill in heaven.

Graduating with honors in 1991, Jennifer, now 18, was ready to embark on her journey into adulthood. Around this time, her family dynamics changed as her mother remarried and they moved to Missoula, Montana's second-largest city. However, Jennifer's eyes were set beyond Montana. She joined a mission group through her church, destined for Mexico. There, she immersed herself in community service, painting and repairing churches, and engaging in outreach programs. Her journal entry from July 11, 1991, reflects her deep sense of purpose and faith, feeling 'in place' and under God's guidance.

Upon returning to Montana, Jennifer was eager to go back to Mexico. She deferred her plans to attend Concordia College in Minnesota upon learning about another mission trip. This new adventure entailed a bike ride from San Diego to Mexico. Determined, she received a Fuji mountain bike as a graduation gift, which solidified her resolve. Despite the initial mission group backing out, Jennifer's tenacity shone through. She decided to undertake the journey alone, much to the concern of her family. Her stepfather, Lyndon James, tried to dissuade her, but Jennifer's mind was made up.

In her journal entry dated September 9th, Jennifer expressed a profound sense of frustration and yearning for understanding. She felt a strong calling to Mexico, yet was met with skepticism and misunderstanding from those around her. This internal conflict was deeply personal, as she grappled with the desire to follow her own path, driven by a sense of divine guidance, versus the expectations and concerns of others. Her writing revealed a deep-seated struggle to articulate her motivations and a plea for divine guidance in the face of loneliness and doubt.

Over the subsequent days, Jennifer's journal entries depicted a young woman wrestling with her decision. She was torn between her ambition to embark on a solo bike trip to San Diego and the real fears and uncertainties that such a journey entailed. By September 16th, a sense of resolution emerged in her writings. She was ready to confront the reality of her situation and inform her loved ones of her definitive plan to leave.

Jennifer's departure from Missoula in late September was a leap into the unknown, armed with essentials including her mountain bike, helmet, two bibles (one in Spanish), a camera, a Walkman, maps, camping gear, clothes, and a modest sum of cash. Her travel plans, though somewhat ambiguous in the media, became clearer through a combination of her journal entries and interviews with her mother. An article in the Missoulian shed light on her intended route: a challenging journey from San Diego to Hermosillo, Mexico, and then onwards to Guadalajara, covering over 1,500 miles.

Early in her trip, Jennifer experienced a pivotal moment. After crossing into Mexico and reaching Tecate, she encountered an acquaintance from previous mission trips. This friend, cognizant of the dangers, advised her against traveling alone through the Mexican desert. Heeding this advice, Jennifer decided to alter her route, opting to traverse the more perilous stretches within the safety of the United States.

Her journey was marked by regular phone calls to her mother, which, coupled with her journal entries, provide a detailed account of her travels. By October 6th, she had crossed back into the United States, camping in Potrero, California. She was still considering whether to continue her journey or to volunteer with the Christian Outreach Appeal (COA) in Tecate.

Her journal entries from early October describe a challenging journey marked by physical exhaustion, mechanical issues, and encounters with both kindness and indifference. Her route took her through Campo, California, where a flat tire and the late hour forced her to halt. An unexpected offer of a ride from a Mexican family allowed her to bypass the daunting mountainous terrain, taking her to El Centro, California.

Following a week-long gap in her journal, Jennifer's last entry on October 14th, just days before her disappearance, surfaced. Her writings during this period reflect a growing disillusionment with the Christian community she encountered and a sense of isolation. Despite these challenges, she continued her journey, eventually reaching Deming, New Mexico, where she made a significant decision to alter her plans.

In her final phone call home on October 17th, Jennifer conveyed a change in tone and intention. No longer planning to head into Mexico, she expressed a longing for her friend Michelle at Concordia College and considered heading to Minnesota instead. Her mother, Lynn, was surprised and somewhat relieved by this change but remained concerned about the challenges of such a journey northwards, especially given the approaching winter.

Jennifer's final journal entries provide insight into her changing perspective. Encounters with various churches left her feeling a sense of obligation rather than genuine Christian love. Her experiences with rudeness and indifference led her to question the state of Christianity in America.

Lynn, worried about the daunting journey ahead, offered to buy Jennifer a bus ticket to Minnesota. However, Jennifer, ever independent, wanted to make the decision on her own. She promised to call her mother from Las Cruces, New Mexico, to finalize her plans.

The days following Jennifer's last call to her mother, Lynn, unfolded with a growing sense of dread. When Jennifer didn't reach out on Lynn's birthday, Saturday, October 19th, the unease transformed into a tangible fear that something was amiss. Lynn initially tried to rationalize the silence, hoping that Jennifer might be in a location without access to a phone. However, as the weekend drew to a close, the sinking realization that something more sinister might have happened began to take hold. This led to the filing of a missing person's report with the Missoula Police Department, who then coordinated with the police in New Mexico.

The response from law enforcement was mixed. While the Las Cruces police showed a willingness to assist, the Deming police appeared less engaged in the case. In a determined effort to find her daughter, Lynn and her husband journeyed to New Mexico in mid-November. They tirelessly scoured Deming, distributing missing person flyers, visiting pawn and bike shops, and searching along major and back roads, hoping for any sign of Jennifer.

Their efforts led them to Jesus Vasquez, a gas station attendant who recalled Jennifer's last known appearance. He provided a detailed description of her attire, her actions at the gas station, and their brief interaction. However, his recollection of her destination—Mexico—contradicted Jennifer's decision to head north, adding to the confusion. Other witnesses' accounts were equally perplexing, with some claiming to have seen Jennifer heading northeast, while others insisted she was southbound, inquiring about the route to Mexico City. The ambiguity of these sightings, compounded by the vagueness of their dates, muddled the timeline of Jennifer's journey.

After an exhaustive six-day search in Deming, Lynn returned home, no closer to unraveling the mystery of her daughter's whereabouts. The rollercoaster of emotions continued for the family. On some days, Lynn clung to the hope that

Jennifer had ventured into Mexico and would eventually contact them, lost in her altruistic pursuits. Other days were overshadowed by darker thoughts of abduction or worse.

Nearly a year later, a crucial discovery was made by two hunters in an area north of Highway 26, near Hatch, New Mexico. The site, an unofficial dumping ground just off a dirt road, yielded some of Jennifer's belongings. This discovery prompted extensive searches by investigators and a Donna Ana-based search and rescue team. While many of Jennifer's possessions were recovered, crucial items like her sleeping bag, bike, and the majority of her money were missing. Only 83 cents and a Mexican peso were found, a stark contrast to the $300.45 she had last accounted for.

The location of these items only deepened the mystery. Jennifer had intended to reach Las Cruces, to the east, not take State Road 26 towards Hatch to the northeast. The discovery raised questions about whether Jennifer had made a navigational error, received misguided directions, or perhaps was taken off her intended path by someone else. John Holguin of the state police, speaking to the Albuquerque Journal, expressed his uncertainty about the situation, highlighting the lack of conclusive evidence pointing either towards Jennifer's whereabouts or any indication of foul play.

As time passed, Jennifer's case gradually grew cold, with few, if any, significant updates after 1992. Despite the lack of new leads, Jennifer's family remained dedicated to keeping her story alive. They returned to New Mexico annually, continuing the search and maintaining close contact with investigators, holding onto the hope that one day the truth about Jennifer's fate would be uncovered.

In October 1998, a determined Lynn and James made an appearance on the Maury show, a platform they hoped would bring renewed attention to Jennifer's case. They sought the insights of a psychic, clinging to any glimmer of hope that might lead to their daughter's whereabouts. Their aspiration to feature Jennifer's story on more widely recognized programs like Unsolved Mysteries, however, remained unfulfilled.

Following their appearance on the show, Lynn received a phone call from a woman who claimed to have encountered Jennifer in San Francisco. This sighting, like several others that emerged over the years, could not be substantiated. Rumors and supposed sightings of Jennifer living in New Mexico also surfaced, but none led to any concrete evidence. Intriguingly, several online sources, including notable ones like the Charlie Project, mentioned Jennifer possibly being in the company of a woman named Teresa. The origin of this detail remains unclear, as there is no available information to explain its basis.

The Deming police, throughout their investigation, never publicly identified a suspect or a person of interest in Jennifer's disappearance. However, in a January 1999 interview with the Great Falls Tribune, Lynn revealed that her family had suspicions about Jesus Vasquez, the gas station attendant in Deming who was reportedly the last person to see Jennifer. Lynn felt strongly that Vasquez might know something more, but he had not been forthcoming in their eyes. This angle, though mentioned, did not gain significant traction in the public domain or among other investigative reports.

As 2021 marked the 30th anniversary of Jennifer's disappearance, the details of her physical appearance and the items she was last seen with remain crucial in the ongoing search. Jennifer Lynn Pentilla was a Caucasian female with blonde hair, blue eyes, standing 5 feet 5 inches tall, and weighing approximately 120 pounds at the time of her disappearance. Distinctive features included a birthmark on her left forearm, a laparotomy scar on her abdomen, and diagonal scars on the tips of her index and middle fingers. Known for wearing glasses, she had a gap between her front teeth and her blood type was O negative. Jennifer was last seen wearing a blue Bum brand sweatshirt over a tank top, denim shorts, socks, brown hiking boots, dog tags with her name and address, a friendship bracelet, a silver ring inscribed with "Love Jesus," and a watch adorned with the Rice Krispies characters Snap, Crackle, and Pop.

Most of her belongings were discovered seven miles outside of Hatch, north of State Road 26. However, her sleeping bag and bike, a white Fuji Sundance with green lettering, engraved with her name and a relative's phone number, and bearing the serial number F9101771, were never found. If alive, Jennifer would be 47 years old today.

For over three decades, the enigma of Jennifer's disappearance has lingered, casting a shadow over her family and the investigators involved in the case. Despite the discovery of her belongings, no major breakthroughs or substantial leads have surfaced. The case, under the jurisdiction of the New Mexico State Police, has inevitably grown cold, with only sporadic, unconfirmed sightings adding to the file.

Lynn, now 70, continues to harbor hope that her daughter might still be somewhere out there. In a heartfelt interview in 2016, she expressed the enduring pain and longing felt by the family, emphasizing their unwavering desire to find Jennifer and bring closure to a mystery that has spanned more than three decades.

Keeshae Jacobs

Keeshae Jacobs, born on a warm summer day, August 6th, 1995, grew up in the historic city of Richmond, Virginia, under the loving care of her single mother, Tony. Their family, though small, was a close-knit and resilient unit, fortified by Tony's unwavering determination and maternal love. Embracing the challenges of single motherhood, Tony juggled various customer service roles, demonstrating a remarkable tenacity in ensuring financial stability and a nurturing home environment for her children.

In this loving household, Tony was more than a mother; she was a pillar of strength and a source of endless support. She cultivated a life for her family that balanced responsibilities with joyous moments. Regular trips to their favorite amusement park, King's Dominion, were a testament to Tony's belief in the importance of leisure and making cherished memories.

Tony's commitment to family extended beyond her immediate circle. She nurtured strong bonds with relatives, instilling a sense of community and belonging in her children. Frequent visits to coastal relatives became a treasured tradition, enriching their lives with a broad sense of family and connection.

Among Tony's children, Keeshae and her sibling Devon shared a remarkably close bond, transcending the usual dynamics of sibling relationships. Their connection was a source of fascination and admiration to all who knew them. Despite their age difference, they supported and cherished each other, illustrating the profound impact of sibling love.

As the years unfolded, Devon, upon completing high school, chose to stay in Richmond, valuing the proximity to his mother and sister. Meanwhile, Keeshae embarked on her high school journey, her bright personality shining through in every endeavor. Joining the cheerleading squad under Tony's guidance, she thrived, her energy and enthusiasm resonating with teammates and peers alike. Throughout these formative years, Keeshae confided in her mother about the trials and tribulations of teenage life, including the complexities of young love. Tony, ever the attentive listener, offered wisdom and comfort, acutely aware of her daughter's trusting nature.

After high school, Keeshae, following in her brother's footsteps, remained in Richmond. During this period, she explored various job opportunities, seeking her true calling. It was her role at a local daycare that resonated deeply with her, her nurturing spirit finding fulfillment in caring for children.

However, the tapestry of their lives was not without its darker threads. In 2016, Devon faced a harrowing experience, an arrest that led to his incarceration, a painful separation that left an indelible mark on the family. Keeshae, particularly, felt the absence of her brother deeply. His eventual release was a moment of profound relief and joy, reuniting the siblings. Devon emerged with a renewed purpose, determined to steer clear of any path that could cause further pain to his beloved sister.

On a crisp autumn night, September 26th, 2016, a seemingly ordinary series of events unfolded in Richmond, Virginia, which would soon unravel into a harrowing mystery. Keeshae Jacobs had plans for a sleepover at a friend's house, a common and unremarkable occurrence for a young woman her age. Leaving her home around 11 p.m., she carried with her the casual excitement of a night spent with friends. Her mother, Tony, ever cautious and caring, had given Keeshae specific instructions: to send a text upon her arrival, ensuring her safe passage.

True to her word, at 11:41 p.m., Keeshae sent that crucial message, concluding with a warm expression of love and the promise to see her mother the following morning. Tony, reassured by her daughter's message, proceeded with her night, unaware of the significance this text message would soon hold. It marked the last communication she would ever receive from Keeshae. Tragically, Keeshae never returned home the next day, and her whereabouts remain unknown.

The bond between Tony and Keeshae was deep and profound. Tony, expecting to hear from her daughter early the next morning, felt a surge of unease when neither a text nor a phone call came. This silence was out of character for Keeshae, who frequently checked in with her mother throughout the day. The concern was shared by Keeshae's older brother, Devon, who was equally close to her. They had plans to cook breakfast together that Tuesday morning, and Devon's initial assumption that Keeshae was merely sleeping in soon turned to worry as the hours ticked by with no word from her.

As the day wore on, Tony, though fraught with worry, had to attend to her work responsibilities. However, her concern intensified with each passing hour that brought no contact from Keeshae. Reaching out to Devon, she found her anxiety mirrored in his response. Together, they attempted numerous calls to Keeshae, only to be met with the disheartening sound of her calls diverting straight to voicemail.

Returning home from work that afternoon to an empty house, Tony's fears escalated. She embarked on a mission to contact all of Keeshae's friends, desperately seeking any clue to her daughter's whereabouts. Yet, none of her friends could provide any information or even speculate where Keeshae might be.

As night fell, Tony's worry transformed into action. She got into her car and drove through the neighborhood, eyes scanning every street and corner for any sign of her daughter. This search, driven by a mother's love and desperation, unfortunately yielded no results. The night seemed to swallow any trace of Keeshae, leaving her family in a state of despair and uncertainty.

In the deep of the night, with the world around her asleep, Tony Jacobs lay awake, tormented by the unknown whereabouts of her daughter, Keeshae. As dawn broke on the following morning, her worry had transformed into determination. She made her way to the Richmond Police Department to report Keeshae missing. What she encountered there was a disheartening indifference that many families of missing black persons have experienced all too frequently. The police brushed off Keeshae's disappearance, suggesting that as an adult, she was entitled to leave home whenever she pleased. But Tony knew her daughter; this uncharacteristic silence was a glaring red flag.

Armed with her conviction, Tony, right there in the precinct, presented the officers with a history of her text and call logs with Keeshae. This digital trail painted a vivid picture of their close relationship, how after graduating from Richmond High School, Keeshae had chosen to stay close to home, often foregoing nights out with friends to be with her family. Even on the night she vanished, after an argument with her boyfriend, it was her mother and brother who had encouraged her to go out.

Returning home from the police station, Tony was visited by some of Keeshae's friends. Initially, they feigned ignorance about her whereabouts post leaving her friend's house. However, they soon revealed a critical piece of information – Keeshae had gone to see a man renting a room on Broad Street in the Church Hill section of Richmond. Confused by their initial reluctance to share this, Tony was nonetheless grateful for the lead.

Tony, fueled by a mother's relentless pursuit of truth, found herself at the doorstep of the Broad Street house. Confronted with the man, Otis Lee Tucker, his story about Keeshae's whereabouts continually shifted, setting off alarm bells for Tony. She called the police, but even they couldn't penetrate his contradictory accounts. Intriguingly, Tucker himself requested a detective, already investigating him for another crime, to search his house, a move that baffled everyone.

Despite the search yielding no concrete results, Keeshae's case began to garner public attention. A press conference on October 4th, 2016, heightened the visibility of her disappearance. The following day brought another twist. Tony received a call from the owner of the house where Keeshae was last seen, inviting her to search the property. While she found nothing of Keeshae's, a disturbing discovery of bloody tissues in a trash can raised more questions than answers.

The Richmond Police Department expanded their search, scouring the neighborhood and nearby Shimoro Park. Yet, all efforts were fruitless in shedding light on Keeshae's fate. In the midst of this heart-wrenching search, Tony was struck by another tragedy – the fatal shooting of her son Devon outside a Richmond motel on January 8th, 2017. The perpetrator, James Henshaw, was apprehended and convicted of involuntary manslaughter, though Devon's death was unrelated to Keeshae's disappearance.

Years passed with no breakthrough, and by the sixth anniversary of Keeshae's disappearance, Tony took a bold step. She publicly named Otis Lee Tucker, the man she believed held the key to her daughter's fate. Tucker's violent history, including an attack on a woman a week before Keeshae vanished, and a later conviction for a murder in Florida, painted a sinister picture, yet no direct evidence linked him to Keeshae.

As the years turned, Tony Jacobs stood undeterred, a testament to a mother's unyielding love and determination. Her quest for the truth about her daughter's disappearance continues, a poignant narrative of hope amidst despair, and the relentless pursuit of justice against seemingly insurmountable odds.

Heather Kullorn

Heather Nicole Kullorn's life began on a spring day, March 9, 1987, in the vibrant city of Saint Louis. She was the cherished daughter of Christine, a mother who embraced the joys and challenges of parenthood with unwavering dedication. While the narrative of Heather's early years seldom mentions her father, it's known that his presence faded from her life when she was just a toddler. Heather was the younger of two siblings, her brother Matthew being three years her senior, which naturally positioned her as the family's beloved youngest member.

From a young age, Heather's personality shone brightly, illuminating the lives of those around her. Described as a whirlwind of energy and spirit, her presence was impossible to ignore. Words like "boisterous" and "spitfire" frequently cropped up when friends and family reminisced about her, painting a picture of a girl with an infectious zest for life. Her vivacious nature was evident in her actions and interactions, marking her as someone who embraced life with both arms.

Heather's early years were characterized by a maturity that belied her age. People often remarked that she seemed like a 12-year-old with the wisdom and poise of someone twice her age. Despite the absence of her father, Heather's life was rich in familial bonds. She was surrounded by aunts, uncles, and cousins, with whom she shared countless cherished moments. These family gatherings were a fertile ground for her nurturing spirit, particularly evident in her love for playing "schoolhouse" with her younger cousins, an early indication of her affinity for caring for children.

Adventure and excitement were never far from Heather's doorstep. She was particularly fond of amusement parks, holding a prized season pass to Six Flags, which she used to satisfy her thrill-seeking side. These outings were not just about the rides; they were a testament to her fearless approach to life and her desire to soak up every experience to the fullest.

Heather's mother, Christine, in conversations with the Saint Louis Post-Dispatch, lovingly described her daughter as a straightforward, attention-loving girl who wasn't afraid to speak her mind. This attribute was an endearing part of her personality, marking her as someone unafraid to be herself.

As Heather transitioned into adolescence, she faced a significant health challenge. Diagnosed with type 1 diabetes in early 1999, she had to adapt to a new routine of twice-daily insulin injections. This condition, unfortunately, led to her missing substantial school time, necessitating a repeat of her sixth-grade year. However, Heather's resilience in the face of this adversity brought her and Christine closer together.

Around this time, Heather's relationship with her mother evolved. They navigated the typical mother-daughter dynamics of the pre-teen years, including a slight rebellious streak in Heather. Yet, it was clear that their bond was strong and loving.

In the realm of friendships and relationships, Heather was equally comfortable with peers her age and adults. She formed a special bond with Dana Madden and Christopher Herbert, friends of the family. Heather's fondness for children was evident in her excitement to babysit Madden and Herbert's baby daughter, a role that allowed her to express her caring nature while asserting her growing independence.

Heather's life in St. Louis was filled with the usual ups and downs of a young girl growing up. She was finding her own identity, experimenting with fashion and makeup, and enjoying the company of her family and friends. Her spirited personality, love for adventure, and caring nature made her a beloved figure in her community.

Unfortunately, the events of July 1999 would bring an abrupt and mysterious end to this vibrant young life. Heather's disappearance from Madden and Herbert's apartment remains a heartbreaking and unsolved mystery. The hours leading up to her disappearance are shrouded in uncertainty and conflicting accounts, leaving more questions than answers.

The apartment where she resided showed no signs of forced entry, yet the scene inside painted a worrying picture. Investigators discovered traces of blood in various locations - on the floor, the couch, and even on the walls, adding a sinister tone to the investigation. The blood's presence extended outside too, with a small patch found in the grass behind the building. At that point, the authorities were in a state of uncertainty about whether the blood belonged to Heather, pending test results. However, they could confidently rule out the blood found outside, thanks to a resident who explained it was his, a result of a dog bite.

The apartment itself seemed to tell a story of disarray. Several items appeared misplaced, although it was unclear whether this was indicative of a theft or a struggle. Among the missing items, a peculiarly described off-white comforter, adorned with faded flowers, caught the investigators' attention. This detail later gained significance in the investigation.

During their neighborhood canvassing, multiple residents reported hearing a baby crying in the early morning hours. Only one person, however, claimed to have witnessed something potentially related to Heather's disappearance. This neighbor, stepping out at around 2 am to walk his dog, reported seeing an unidentified man exiting Heather's apartment. This man was carrying what seemed to be a sleeping child, wrapped in a white comforter. The neighbor's account was particularly concerning as he noted the child's bare legs dangling from the blanket, shoeless. This testimony added an urgent and distressing dimension to the search for Heather.

Further complicating the situation was Heather's medical condition. She required daily insulin injections, but all her medical supplies were left behind, intensifying concerns for her physical well-being. While the witness provided some details, his vision impairment, being legally blind without his glasses, which he wasn't wearing at the time, meant the description of the man was vague at best.

The police, sensing the gravity of the situation, enlisted the assistance of the FBI within the first 24 hours. Suspicion fell on Christopher Herbert, Heather's father, who had reported her missing. Herbert was detained on an unrelated traffic violation, during which time he gave conflicting accounts of his whereabouts on the night Heather disappeared. His initial claim of driving a friend home was soon retracted, replaced with a story of partying by the Mississippi River. These inconsistencies in his story raised eyebrows.

Meanwhile, Christine, Heather's mother, was in anguish over her daughter's disappearance. She strongly believed that either Herbert or Madden, or both, knew more than they were letting on. She mobilized friends and family in a city-wide search, distributing missing person flyers extensively. The community rallied around the search, with local businesses offering a $10,000 reward for information leading to Heather's whereabouts or an arrest.

In a twist, the police discovered a methamphetamine manufacturing operation in a garage linked to Herbert, suggesting a possible connection to Heather's disappearance. Heather might have known about the illegal activities and become a target due to fear of exposure. This theory was bolstered by the involvement of Mike Mason, a friend of Herbert's, and Dana Madden, who were also implicated in the drug operation.

Despite intense investigations, no concrete leads emerged. The frustration was palpable among both the investigators and Heather's family. The discovery of a white blanket near the Mississippi River added a glimmer of hope, but it was quickly extinguished when Madden confirmed it wasn't the missing comforter.

The case took a grim turn when, by July 19th, the police publicly expressed fears that Heather might have been a victim of homicide, though they stopped short of naming any suspects. The investigation continued, expanding to areas and individuals connected to Heather and her family. However, despite the dedicated efforts of a team of seasoned investigators, no significant breakthroughs were made.

Eleven days had passed since Heather mysteriously disappeared, and the atmosphere was tense with concern and unanswered questions. The police, determined to unravel the mystery, announced that the Major Case Squad would relentlessly pursue the investigation until they reached a resolution. Chief Lowry, during this announcement, shared some significant revelations that had come to light.

The investigation had uncovered a troubling web of connections. It turned out that several individuals in Heather's life were entangled in the dangerous world of methamphetamine, either as users or producers. While specific names were withheld from the public, it was disclosed that three of Heather's acquaintances had been arrested on drug-related charges, and there were expectations that another nine would soon face a similar fate.

The police had managed to narrow down their list of potential suspects to just a few, a "handful" as they described it. Among them, a prime suspect had emerged, though their identity remained undisclosed. This individual had notably failed a polygraph test, adding a layer of suspicion around them. The investigative team had also questioned several of Heather's family members more than once, understanding the importance of scrutinizing every possible angle.

On the 27th of July, a new, chilling dimension to the case was revealed. The police strongly believed that Heather's abduction, and the likelihood of her murder, was intricately linked to a major methamphetamine ring, sprawling from Saint Louis to the Missouri Boot Heel. This revelation was accompanied by the disturbing detail that someone involved in this drug ring was manufacturing meth in the garage of the apartment complex on the night Heather was taken.

This complex web of crime and mystery deepened when the Saint Charles County-based rescue team planned a thorough search of the Mississippi River near the park where a blanket had been found, hoping for any sign of Heather. Although this search, conducted on July 28th, didn't yield results, it underscored the seriousness and scope of the investigation.

The case took a more convoluted turn when Herbert, a person of interest, gave conflicting stories about his whereabouts on the night of the abduction. Initially, he claimed to have been partying by the river, indulging in methamphetamine. However, court documents later revealed a different story. Herbert admitted to being in the apartment complex garage, involved in cooking meth. He claimed to have left around 10:30 PM to get more supplies and didn't return until six hours later. Upon his return, he found Heather missing and noticed blood in various places in the apartment. His account included a mention of an associate, a man dating a woman who owned a red BMW, a vehicle Herbert admitted to having stolen from previously.

The investigation found its way to this BMW, which was believed to be directly involved in Heather's kidnapping. The police secured a warrant to search the vehicle, though the outcomes of this search were not disclosed.

As time passed, the case became increasingly complex and elusive. Investigators sought assistance from the National Center for the Analysis of Violent

Crime, part of the FBI, in a bid to develop a profile of the suspect. Despite the growing despair, Sergeant Vilcek expressed a continued hope for a resolution.

The community rallied around Heather's family, with friends and family holding a church service 130 days after her disappearance. Heather's mother, Christine, expressed a relentless determination to find her daughter, refusing to accept the possibility of a tragic outcome.

As months turned into years, the case saw ups and downs, including a false lead when remains were found in 2002, which were later confirmed not to be Heather's.

The enduring hope of Christine Kullorn, mother of Heather Nicole Kullorn, was a testament to a mother's unwavering love, even in the face of overwhelming despair. Each month, as friends and family gathered at Christine's mother's grave, particularly poignant on what would have been Heather's 16th birthday, the toll of the years without knowing her daughter's fate became increasingly evident. Christine's heartfelt expressions, shared with the Post Dispatch, revealed the intensifying pain with each passing birthday and holiday. The weight of the unknown and the feeling of waging a seemingly losing battle were palpable in her words.

In the midst of this emotional turmoil, the Richmond Heights Police Chief, Ron Pfeiffer, remained actively involved in the case, consistently receiving tips and maintaining the investigation. His startling acknowledgment of having a suspect in mind, yet lacking the crucial evidence for a breakthrough, added a layer of complexity and frustration to the ongoing mystery.

April 2003 marked a significant moment when the Sean Hornbeck Foundation, named after another abducted child, Sean Hornbeck, extended its support to Heather's case. The foundation, which was dedicated to assisting in searches for missing children and supporting their families, sent search dogs to a location in St. Louis County based on a tip Christine received. Although this search did not yield results for Heather, the foundation's efforts, including the "Sitting with an Angel" program, which installed benches with information about missing children, highlighted Heather's case. The first bench dedicated in this program was in honor of Heather.

The eventual discovery and rescue of Sean Hornbeck in January 2007, and the arrest of his captor, Mike Devlin, was a moment of mixed emotions for Christine. While elated for Sean's parents, her own daughter's case remained unresolved. The Jefferson County Sheriff's Department, in an effort to revive public interest, included Heather in a rally for missing people in August 2008. Despite these efforts, the case's visibility waned over time.

Fifteen years after Heather's disappearance, on July 15, 2014, the community's engagement had diminished, yet investigators remained vigilant, confident they were close to a breakthrough. Christine, however, expressed her dissatisfaction with their approach, feeling more could be done. Her relentless efforts to keep Heather's story alive, through flyers and conversations, reflected her deep commitment to seeking justice for her daughter.

Tragically, Christine Kullorn passed away on December 16, 2017, without witnessing the resolution of her daughter's case. Her obituary poignantly listed Heather as a survivor, a symbol of her never-fading hope. That same year, Detective Mike Brown revealed in a radio interview the existence of two suspects, both with criminal histories, yet without sufficient evidence for an arrest. The hope was that new evidence or a crucial tip might finally bring justice for Heather and closure for her family.

Heather Kullorn, at the time of her disappearance, was a young girl with distinct physical characteristics, suffering from Type 1 diabetes, a condition that required regular insulin shots. Sadly, her medical supplies were left behind, adding another layer of urgency and concern to her disappearance. Today, if alive, Heather would be 33 years old, and age-progressed photographs have been circulated in hopes of aiding the investigation.

The case of Heather Nicole Kullorn remains a haunting reminder of the fragility of life and the enduring pain of not knowing. It underscores the reality that there are individuals who possess vital information, individuals who could end decades of anguish for Heather's family. Christine's plea, echoing through the years, remains relevant: anyone with information, no matter how insignificant it may seem, has the power to make a profound difference. It's not just about solving a case; it's about bringing peace to a family torn apart by tragedy and ensuring that justice is served, even posthumously, for Christine Kullorn's enduring fight for her daughter.

Teresa Lynn Butler

The story of Teresa Lynn Butler is a deeply intriguing one, woven into the fabric of small-town America. Born on November 26, 1970, in the quaint town of Gideon, Missouri, Teresa's life was emblematic of the simplicity and close-knit community spirit that small towns are known for. Gideon, nestled in the southeastern part of Missouri, often referred to as the "Bootheel," is a place where everyone knows everyone else. With a modest population of just over a thousand people, spread across 1.8 square miles, it's the kind of town where secrets are hard to keep, and personal stories are shared like communal treasures.

Teresa, as those who knew her fondly recall, was the epitome of kindness and warmth. Amy Lacy, who had the privilege of calling Teresa a friend since fourth grade, paints a picture of a woman whose presence was like a gentle breeze on a warm summer day. Teresa's generosity knew no bounds, her sense of humor was as infectious as her kindness, and she had this uncanny ability to make anyone feel at ease. This was a woman who embodied the very essence of what it means to be a caring, loving human being.

Amy, driven by a deep sense of loss and a burning need for answers, set up a website dedicated to Teresa's case. In her heartfelt tribute, Amy reminisced about their school days, how Teresa, though quiet, was immensely popular and loved by all. Voted the most courteous in their senior year, Teresa's love for her family, her unwavering dedication to her husband Gary Dale Butler, and her adoration for her two boys, were the cornerstones of her life.

The tranquility of Teresa's life in Risco, a town even smaller than Gideon, was shattered on January 24, 2006. At 35, Teresa vanished, leaving behind a trail of questions and few clues. On that fateful day, her usual routine gave no hint of the mystery that was about to unfold. She spent her day as she always did, caring for her family and engaging in simple pleasures. But as night fell and her husband Dale went to his overnight shift, the fabric of normalcy began to unravel.

The last known interactions with Teresa are etched in the minds of those who loved her. Sara Buchanan, Teresa's sister-in-law, recalls their last conversation, mundane yet now precious in its normalcy. The topic of a gel for a breakout, a plan to meet the next morning – these were the simple threads of a life that was about to be irrevocably altered.

Dale, returning from his shift, was greeted not by the warmth of his wife but by a silence that screamed of something amiss. The discovery of their sons, alone and in distress, set off a chain of events that would engulf the small community in a mystery that persists to this day. The house, outwardly undisturbed, hid the unsettling truth of Teresa's disappearance. The missing items – a PlayStation, a GameCube, a flashlight, a video camera, and Teresa's purse and phone – seemed to tell a story of theft, yet left more questions than answers.

The most disturbing clues, however, were not what was missing, but what was left behind. Teresa's leather jacket, a constant companion in her life, lay untouched. Her wedding rings, found in an unusual spot, spoke of an abrupt disruption. And the broken key in the lock – a silent witness to an unknown struggle.

As authorities delved into the mystery, the theories multiplied. Was it a robbery gone wrong? An abduction? Or something more personal? The presence of foreign DNA in the house added another layer to the puzzle. Dale, despite being scrutinized, was cleared by the authorities, his alibi standing firm against the tides of suspicion.

The timeline of her vanishing, particularly between 10:00 and 11:00 p.m., remains shrouded in uncertainty, sparking numerous theories and speculations. With scant evidence at hand, authorities struggled to pin down the exact moment of Teresa's disappearance, turning their attention to her cell phone records for potential clues.

In a twist that deepened the mystery, Teresa's cell phone records revealed two enigmatic calls made after she was last seen alive at 10:00 p.m. The first, at 3:16 a.m., was to a number in Gideon, her hometown. The recipient of this call, when contacted by authorities, expressed his bewilderment, stating that he had no recollection of the phone ringing and only noticed a missed call later. No connection between this individual and Teresa or her family could be established.

The second call, equally baffling, was made to a residence in Clarkton, Missouri. This call reached two elderly ladies, who reported answering the phone to silence before hanging up. They, too, had no knowledge of Teresa or her family. These calls, intriguingly, were made to numbers within the same county, sharing the area code 573. This coincidence fueled theories ranging from accidental misdials by Teresa herself to deliberate actions by a potential abductor.

The Butler home's proximity to the number 8 drainage ditch added another layer to the search efforts. Despite extensive searches including floating the ditch, using four-wheelers, helicopters, and cadaver dogs, no trace of Teresa was found. Jim Duck of Outback Riders, a non-profit search and rescue organization, expressed his frustration at the lack of leads despite their extensive efforts.

Amidst the growing despair, Teresa's family sought answers from unconventional sources, including Carol Pate, an alleged psychic. While the details of Pate's insights remain undisclosed, Teresa's brother Don conveyed the family's frustration with the lack of progress in the official investigation and their comfort in Pate's professionalism.

As investigators delved deeper into Teresa's personal life, they uncovered a potential lead involving Gary's ex-wife, who reportedly had a contentious relationship with Teresa. While some speculated her involvement in Teresa's disappearance, no concrete evidence emerged to support this theory.

Adding to the enigma was a mysterious letter, mentioned by Dale, Teresa's husband, which purportedly held significant information regarding the case. However, the contents of this letter have remained a closely guarded secret, adding to the labyrinth of unanswered questions surrounding Teresa's fate.

Sheriff Stevens made a pivotal public declaration, acknowledging for the first time his firm belief that foul play played a significant role in the mysterious disappearance of Teresa. His conviction was not just a mere suggestion; he expressed absolute certainty. When probed about the possibility of Teresa's children having witnessed the incident, Stevens expressed his thoughts empathetically, noting that while the children might hold some answers, their young age might hinder their ability to articulate these insights. Despite this, his optimism remained unshaken, holding onto hope for a resolution.

Dale, alongside Teresa's family, engaged in heartfelt public appeals, earnestly hoping that someone would step forward with crucial information. Teresa's mother, Linda, shared her profound grief and confusion in a heartfelt interview, expressing the deep void left by Teresa's absence. She reminisced about their regular visits and the painful realization that she would never again celebrate Christmas with her daughter. This sentiment underscored the family's frustration with the limited media attention Teresa's case had garnered. Despite reaching out to numerous news outlets, they felt overlooked, attributing this to their financial status and the area's economic condition. However, Teresa's significance to them was immeasurable.

As the investigation into Teresa's disappearance continued, police were inundated with hundreds of tips and reported sightings. One particular sighting at a local gas station sparked interest, but the lack of clarity in the surveillance footage thwarted any definitive identification. A breakthrough seemed imminent a year and a half later with the discovery of a camcorder. A local drug dealer claimed he received it as payment and later realized its potential connection to Teresa's case. However, the camcorder was found without a tape and with an illegible serial number, complicating the verification process.

Sheriff Stevens shared insights into the investigation, mentioning an individual who traded illegal drugs for the camcorder. Despite this lead, the authorities could not conclusively rely on this information. They continued to explore various suspects, keeping all possibilities open.

The case also raised the question of whether Teresa's disappearance was linked to a robbery intended to finance a drug deal. Stevens hinted at a potential connection between the drug dealer and Teresa's case. He speculated that Teresa might have hidden her rings under the couch due to discomfort with certain individuals in her home, suggesting a possible connection between her and the intruders.

Dale, when questioned about the possibility of a break-in, expressed his doubts about a forced entry, suggesting a more complex scenario. Lead investigator Chris Hensley highlighted the significance of an unscrewed light bulb, potentially indicating a deliberate attempt to avoid detection during the crime.

Several theories have emerged, ranging from Teresa voluntarily leaving to being involved in illegal activities or being abducted during a robbery. The lack of forced entry and signs of struggle have fueled speculation, with some suspecting her husband, Dale, despite his alibi. The robbery theory posits that the abductors took Teresa to prevent her from identifying them, while another theory suggests abduction was the primary motive, and the robbery was incidental.

As the years progress, advances in technology and investigative techniques offer a glimmer of hope that new evidence might emerge, shedding light on Teresa Butler's fate. This resolution, albeit potentially grim, could provide her family with the much-needed comfort and closure. The enduring mystery of what happened to Teresa, a beloved mother, daughter, and sister, remains a poignant reminder of the complexities and unpredictabilities of such cases.

Patricia Carter and Kelly Moriarty

Kelly Michelle Moriarty's story begins on a sunny Sunday, June 3rd, 1973, in the quaint upstate village of Millbrook, New York, nestled in the heart of Dutchess County. Born to Bud and Grace, Kelly was the cherished fourth child and the only daughter in a lively household buzzing with the energy of three older brothers. Her childhood in Millbrook was picturesque, with the village's close-knit community and abundant natural beauty providing a perfect backdrop for her formative years.

From a young age, Kelly was known for her vibrant personality, one that radiated joy and warmth. Her infectious laugh became her signature, a sound that could light up a room and bring smiles to the faces of friends and family alike. She was the kind of person who naturally drew others towards her with her unwavering positivity and zest for life.

Kelly's brothers, especially Brendan, fondly recall how she was always an eager companion in their adventures, never hesitating to tag along and join in whatever they were doing. This was more than just sibling camaraderie; it was the forging of unbreakable bonds and the creation of cherished memories.

Athletics played a significant role in Kelly's upbringing. Her natural athletic prowess was evident from a young age, and she quickly developed a passion for sports. Her father once remarked that among all his children, Kelly stood out as the most gifted athlete. This was no small praise, considering the athletic talents of her siblings. Millbrook, with its abundant outdoor spaces and emphasis on community sports, was the perfect place for Kelly to hone her skills.

Kelly's love for softball was particularly strong. She wasn't just a player; she was a force to be reckoned with on the field. Her ability to hit home runs and make exceptional plays was nothing short of remarkable. Throughout the late 1980s and early 1990s, Kelly's name frequently appeared in local newspapers, praised for her hard work and extraordinary abilities. She played for the Debs, a fast-pitch club committed to developing players both on and off the field, and her performances in various tournaments were nothing short of stellar. The Poughkeepsie Journal once reported her outstanding performance at the East Fishkill tournament, where she not only had three hits in the finals but was also named the MVP of the entire tournament.

Kelly's high school years saw her continue to excel in sports, particularly softball, where her batting average was an impressive .460. She balanced her athletic achievements with academic success, maintaining good grades and forming lasting friendships. Her friends, years later, would fondly reminisce about the wonderful times they shared with Kelly, a testament to the lasting impact she had on those around her.

In 1990, as Kelly approached her 17th birthday, her family relocated to the sunnier climes of Florida, settling in the vibrant community of St. Petersburg. Here, she enrolled in St. Petersburg Catholic High School, where she continued to shine in her athletic pursuits. Despite her obvious talents, Kelly remained undecided about her future career path, moving through various jobs, including a stint in bank security, while still playing softball in adult leagues. Her parents, ever her staunchest supporters, rarely missed her games, demonstrating their unwavering belief in her abilities.

As she navigated her late teens and early twenties, Kelly faced a personal revelation that she felt compelled to share with her family: she was gay. This admission, particularly in a family with more conservative values, was a significant moment for Kelly. Her brother Brendan later shared with the Plant City Observer how this was a challenging yet important step for Kelly, signifying her commitment to living authentically.

Kelly's journey into adulthood was marked by her fierce independence and strong sense of privacy. She was known for her ability to engage in deep, meaningful conversations, but also for her firm boundaries regarding her personal life. Her coming out was a moment of vulnerability and courage, and according to her family, it brought them even closer, reinforcing the bond of trust and acceptance within the family unit.

Over the years, Kelly moved around Florida, living in places like Tampa, Bradenton, Gulfport, and St. Petersburg, but always staying within close reach of her family. In her mid-thirties, Kelly discovered a new passion that would shape her career path: massage therapy. This new direction seemed to resonate deeply with her, providing a sense of purpose and fulfillment.

In 2009, at the age of 36, Kelly's life took a significant turn when she met Doris Patricia Carter, a woman who would deeply influence her life's trajectory. They met at Georgie's Alibi, a popular gay bar in St. Petersburg, known for its lively atmosphere and inclusive vibe. Doris, or Pat as she preferred, was the widow of William Ed Carter, a former Hillsborough County sheriff's deputy. Together, they had built a successful business, Carter's Cast Nets, which Pat continued to run after Ed's passing. The business's success had allowed Pat to amass a comfortable financial situation, owning a home and land in Plant City, Florida.

Pat, having spent over three decades with her late husband, found herself seeking companionship and love again. In a heart-to-heart with her brother Charles, she revealed that she was gay, a revelation that came as a surprise but was met with support and happiness from her family. Charles later shared with Crime Watch Daily how Pat felt she had been gay all her life and was now experiencing a newfound happiness.

When Kelly and Pat met, there was an instant connection, a spark that quickly evolved into a deep and passionate relationship. They spent considerable time together, with Pat staying at Kelly's apartment and vice versa. Their bond was strong, and they became a familiar and beloved couple at Georgie's Alibi, the place that had brought them together.

Kelly's journey towards becoming a massage therapist was a leap of hope and ambition. She enrolled at the Florida College of Natural Medicine, driven by a passion to heal and help others. This was a significant turning point in her life, marking the beginning of a new chapter filled with learning and personal growth.

Meanwhile, Pat's life was taking a different turn. Her daughter Stacy, along with her husband Anthony Mural and their daughter, faced financial turmoil following the foreclosure of their home. This led them to move in with Pat in Plant City, a decision that brought its own set of challenges. Pat, who cherished her private space, found herself in a dilemma. Her natural inclination was to support her family, but the invasion of her personal space was a source of considerable stress. This was a tough period for Pat, as she grappled with her desire to help her daughter and the need to maintain her own peace.

As the situation at Pat's home grew more complex, Kelly's presence added another layer to the already strained dynamics. Stacy and Anthony harbored negative opinions about Kelly, viewing her as someone out to exploit Pat financially. This perception might have been influenced by an incident where Pat gifted Kelly a 1998 black Cadillac Catera, a gesture that perhaps raised eyebrows.

The family tensions reached a boiling point when Pat felt compelled to seek legal protection against her own daughter and son-in-law. She described an alarming incident where she was pushed out of her chair, causing injury. This was a cry for help, a sign of how dire the situation had become. Yet, 12 days later, Pat withdrew the petition, leaving the court without the opportunity to establish a more permanent solution.

During this turbulent time, Kelly was finding success in her studies. She excelled in her massage therapy courses, a testament to her dedication and newfound purpose. Her family, who supported her financially, saw this as a turning point in her life. However, Kelly was private about her relationship with Pat, often avoiding questions from her family. This secrecy added an element of mystery to their relationship.

Despite the perceived calm in Kelly and Pat's relationship, Stacy reported frequent loud arguments and fights between the two. This was partially corroborated by court documents, revealing a tumultuous relationship. Pat even filed for protection against Kelly, alleging physical and financial abuse, only for the petition to be dismissed later due to lack of evidence.

Kelly, in turn, filed her own petition against Pat, painting a picture of a controlling and abusive partner. However, she too withdrew her petition, citing work commitments. These legal battles suggested a relationship fraught with conflict and misunderstanding.

As the relationship continued, Kelly contemplated a future that diverged from Pat's. She dreamed of returning to New York to start her own business after completing her courses, a plan that did not seem to include Pat. This hinted at an impending separation post-holidays, a future that never materialized as both women mysteriously disappeared before the year's end.

The situation with Pat, Stacy, and Anthony deteriorated further. Pat sought to evict them from her home, citing prolonged and undesirable occupancy. In a counter-move, Stacy and Anthony questioned Pat's mental health and expressed concerns about Kelly's financial influence over her.

Stacy's saga with Kelly and Pat unfolded like a suspenseful mystery novel, laced with unforeseen twists and complex relationships. It all began when

Stacy shared with ABC her suspicion that the eviction petition against her was a direct consequence of the pressure exerted by Kelly. This suspicion was rooted in the fact that Stacy had previously lodged a complaint against Kelly for elderly financial exploitation with the Department of Children and Families.

As the calendar pages turned to November, the holiday season started to blossom. Thanksgiving, a time traditionally spent in the warmth of family gatherings, was approaching, with this year's celebration slated for Thursday, November 24th. Kelly, who typically spent these festive times with her family, often at her brother's house, made an unexpected decision this year. In a heartfelt phone conversation with her mother, she revealed her plans to spend Thanksgiving not with her family but with Pat, at her home in Plant City. Furthermore, Kelly shared that the coming Christmas would be celebrated at her apartment, with Pat joining her.

The Thanksgiving celebration, according to reports, went smoothly. A few days later, in late November or early December, Grace, Kelly's mother, had what would be her final conversation with her daughter. They reminisced about Thanksgiving and looked forward to Christmas. At that time, there were no signs of trouble or cause for concern.

However, a dramatic turn of events began to unfold on Thursday, December 15th. That was the day when the court granted Pat's petition to evict Stacy and Anthony. This legal action should have propelled the eviction process forward, but strangely, it didn't. Stacy and Anthony continued to reside in Pat's house on McLin Drive. Even more mysteriously, that same Thursday marked the last time anyone saw Kelly and Pat alive. Despite their sudden disappearance on December 15th, no missing person's report was filed for over a month.

During this perplexing period, Pat's friends and Kelly's family were oblivious to their disappearances. Stacy and Anthony, still living in Pat's home, did not reach out to authorities regarding Pat or Kelly's whereabouts.

The following ten days saw two different law enforcement agencies stumble upon clues that, unbeknownst to them, were intricately linked to the missing women. On Monday, December 19th, a deputy from the Manatee County Sheriff's Office discovered an abandoned black 1998 Cadillac Catera parked on State Road 62 in Parish. The car, belonging to Kelly Moriarty, was in good condition, showing no signs of damage or an accident. However, since no missing person's report had been filed yet, the car was simply red-tagged for removal, a process that would not begin until ten days later, on December 29th.

Just two days before the car's removal, another grim discovery was made in Saint Petersburg, about 20 miles northwest of where the car had been found. On the morning of December 27th, a Canadian family on vacation in Saint Petersburg stumbled upon a human leg washed ashore on a beach. The leg, severed at the thigh and ankle with the foot removed, presented a chilling mystery. Despite the absence of obvious trauma, except where the cuts were made, investigators noted mysterious marks circling the upper thigh. The Tampa Bay Times reported that Detective Mike Pewts of the Saint Petersburg Police Department acknowledged the complexity of determining the leg's origin due to the bay's extensive shipping channels.

In the ensuing days, the police conducted extensive searches both in the water and along the shoreline, but no additional evidence was found. The leg's mutilation pointed towards a likely connection to a homicide. Detective Pewts informed the Tampa Bay Times that the medical examiner's office had ascertained that the severing of the leg was done by a human using a cutting tool, not an animal attack. However, identifying the leg's owner proved challenging. The leg, believed to have belonged to a heavyset white woman based on its shaven state, had no DNA matches in the system. It was estimated to have been in the water for no more than 72 hours.

The case took a significant turn on January 27, 2012, a month after the leg's discovery, when Brendan Moriarty, Kelly's brother, received a concerning phone call. Kelly's landlord, having not seen her since December and with rent overdue, contacted Brendan, listed as the emergency contact on Kelly's lease. Brendan's subsequent visit to Kelly's apartment revealed an eerie scene: a well-kept apartment, but evidently unoccupied for some time. A Christmas tree still stood with presents underneath, a newspaper from December 8th lay on the couch, and expired milk dated December 23rd was in the refrigerator. Alarmed, Brendan filed a missing person's report for Kelly.

When police inquired about the last time Kelly had been seen or heard from, it was established that she had spoken to her mother after Thanksgiving, but there had been no contact since early December at the latest. Kelly's family explained that it was not unusual for her to be out of touch for extended periods. Grace, her mother, told the Plant City Observer that Kelly, at 38 years old, was independent and their communication could sometimes be sporadic.

In a mysterious and perplexing turn of events, investigators uncovered an enigmatic and somewhat baffling situation in a house that seemed to be a scene straight out of a suspense novel. Here, they found Stacy and Anthony, an unexpected discovery considering that just over a month before, a judge had ruled in Pat's favor to evict them. This revelation set the stage for an intricate web of mysteries and unanswered questions.

As the investigation delved deeper, Stacy shared her last memory of seeing her mother and Kelly, which coincidentally was on the very day the eviction judgment was passed – Thursday, December 15th. The details surrounding that day were murky and somewhat inconsistent. Stacy recounted an argument between Kelly and Pat, and from there, the stories diverged. Some reports suggested that Stacy witnessed the pair leaving in Kelly's Cadillac, while others claimed Stacy had gone to bed, and upon waking, found her mother, Kelly, and the car all missing.

The situation grew more complex when questioned about the lack of a missing person's report. Stacy's explanation mirrored the Moriarty family's sentiments, citing her mother's habitual disappearances and stays with Kelly as the reason for no immediate concern. However, the plot thickened on January 28th when Kelly filed an official missing person's report for her mother.

Detectives soon discovered Kelly's car abandoned in a Manatee County impound lot since December 29th. The car, found locked and in working order, suggested an ominous possibility – it might have been deliberately abandoned by someone other than Kelly. A curious note emerged from Detective Tom Dirks in a Crime Watch Daily interview. While initially reported that no evidence was found in the car, Dirks hinted at the collection of multiple items from the vehicle, the details of which he could not disclose.

Amidst this developing investigation, unaware of the grisly discovery in Saint Petersburg – a severed leg – the authorities were still approaching this as a missing person's case. However, a chilling discovery in early February connected the dots in a way no one had anticipated. The Hillsborough County Sheriff's Office found the body of a deceased male in Brandon, partially mutilated, but notably, not missing a leg. This prompted authorities to consider a potential link to the severed leg found earlier.

Following an intuitive hunch, investigators obtained DNA samples from Kelly's mother and Pat's daughter. Three weeks later, a significant breakthrough occurred: the Pinellas County Medical Examiner positively identified the leg as belonging to Kelly Moriarty. While the cause of death remained a mystery, and Kelly's body was still missing, the indication was clear – foul play was likely involved.

The case now escalated into a desperate search for Pat, with Hillsborough County Sheriff's spokesman Larry McKinnon expressing a bleak yet hopeful perspective. The investigation spanned across three counties, each focusing on different aspects: Hillsborough on finding Pat, Manatee on locating Kelly and examining the car, and Saint Petersburg on gathering information about the women's disappearance. The National Oceanic and Atmospheric Administration even joined to leverage their expertise in understanding where Kelly's leg might have entered the water.

The Moriarty family, grappling with the tragic reality, issued a heart-wrenching statement, pleading for privacy and justice for Kelly. In stark contrast, Pat's family became less cooperative as the investigation deepened, especially when questions arose about Stacy and Pat's strained relationship, including past legal disputes and the eviction.

Amidst these developments, detectives turned their attention to Anthony Brigitzer and Kelly Rozier, arrested on December 26th in a case that seemed eerily connected. Their vehicle contained suspicious items, including blood-stained hatchets, which later analysis suggested could be linked to Kelly's dismemberment.

In a harrowing twist of events, a further probe into the case revealed the chilling acts of Brigitzer, who was found to have viciously assaulted 70-year-old Mary Corbett before his apprehension. This attack was particularly disturbing as Brigitzer, who was employed as a handyman, had used this position to gain access to Corbett's home. There, he unleashed a horrifying assault, deploying a stun gun against the elderly woman before restraining her and proceeding to rob her. This heinous act led to additional charges against Brigitzer, including assault, kidnapping, fraud, and dealing in stolen property.

Despite rigorous efforts, investigators hit a dead end in linking Brigitzer to Kelly or Pat, two other individuals embroiled in this complex case. With no substantial suspects, no discernible crime scene, and no trace of Pat, the focus of the investigation started to shift towards Stacy and Anthony. This change in direction was spurred by certain alarming revelations. For instance, detectives noted that Anthony harbored a deep-seated animosity towards both Kelly and his mother-in-law. Coupled with existing legal disputes between Pat and the couple, these factors raised significant suspicions, although, as

Larry McKinnon from CBS Tampa Bay pointed out, these were not conclusive indicators of their involvement in any homicide.

In a quest for clarity, investigators orchestrated a thorough search of the McLin Drive home, ten months following the last sighting of Pat and Kelly. Stacy, showing a willingness to cooperate, allowed the search. The forensics team, along with deputies, meticulously scoured the home, employing techniques like luminol spraying to detect traces of blood and gathering various fibers. While the specifics of the evidence collected remained undisclosed, some of it was dispatched for further lab analysis.

Amidst these developments, the Moriarty family, grappling with the unknown and seeking closure, announced a $5,000 reward for information leading to an arrest and conviction. Kelly's brother Brendan poignantly expressed the family's torment, highlighting the excruciating pain of not knowing and their desperate need for answers.

The family also harbored a strong belief that both Kelly and Pat were likely deceased and speculated that their demise occurred in or near Plant City, based on the last known locations of their cell phones. They further theorized that Kelly's abandoned Cadillac was a deliberate misdirection by the perpetrator.

As time marched on, the case experienced frustrating stagnation. Investigators, honing in on Stacy and Anthony, delved into their backgrounds and scrutinized their activities around the time of the disappearances. However, the findings from these inquiries remained largely under wraps. Sheriff's spokesman Larry McKinnon lamented the incomplete nature of the evidence, acknowledging that while they had pieces of the puzzle, they lacked crucial elements to draw definitive conclusions.

Amidst official investigations, Kelly's father Bud embarked on a personal quest for truth, his efforts culminating in a letter to the Tampa Bay Times. In this letter, he shared his conviction about the involvement of Doris Carter's daughter and son-in-law in the case, theorizing about the possible fate of the women.

Years passed with minimal progress in solving the mystery. In December 2014, three years after the last sighting of Kelly and Pat, detectives admitted to accumulating new evidence and information but not enough to press charges. Searches continued, and investigative files grew, yet the evidence remained largely circumstantial.

Major Yura from the Hillsborough County Sheriff's Office noted the focus on Stacy and Anthony Morale, citing their lack of cooperation as a hindrance to the investigation. Intriguingly, Stacy's cell phone records and her actions, such as accessing her mother's safe deposit box, raised further questions. In response to inquiries, Stacy suggested that the crime might have been drug-related and implied that Kelly might have been influencing her mother for financial gain.

Stacy firmly rejected any involvement in the mysterious crime, emphasizing her certainty about not being a part of it. She passionately expressed that the situation was more complex than it appeared and stressed her deep love and sense of responsibility towards her mother. In the ensuing years, Bud, the father, relentlessly pursued justice for his daughter's case and Pat's disappearance. He developed a close bond with Charles Wade, Pat's brother, but couldn't hide his disappointment with the sluggish pace of the official investigation. Despite claims from the police of regular contact, Bud felt left in the dark since the initial stages of the inquiry. He emphasized the critical need for an arrest to advance the case, acknowledging the irrevocable loss of their daughter and their continuous struggle for closure.

Bud raised questions about Stacy and Anthony's apparent lack of cooperation with the investigators, puzzled by their seeming indifference to resolving the case, especially considering Stacy's connection to her mother. By March 2017, after five and a half years of tireless effort, Bud and his wife Grace felt they had hit an impasse. They publicly implored for more information, believing that just one more clue could crack the case wide open. That same month, "Crime Watch Daily" aired two segments on the case, where Charles Wade voiced suspicions about his niece Stacy's involvement, suggesting a financial motive.

Grace relayed that Stacy had informed investigators about an argument between Pat and Kelly on the night they vanished. Stacy had speculated that Kelly might have killed Pat, a theory that appeared odd given that Kelly was the confirmed homicide victim. Bud added that Anthony was rumored to have sold Pat's jewelry and several guns shortly after their disappearance. Brendan, another family member, expressed his family's frustration with the stalled progress in the investigation, highlighting the distressing fact that the perpetrator remained at large.

Sadly, over the next four years, the case saw no significant advancements, with sporadic references to Stacy and Anthony as persons of interest by law enforcement. Bud Moriarty, who dedicated his life to finding answers, passed away in 2019 without seeing the resolution he so desperately sought. Now, the responsibility of seeking justice rests with the Moriarty's three sons, as they continue the quest to uncover the truth about their sister, Kelly Moriarty, and Doris Patricia Carter.

Kelly and Pat were last seen alive in Plant City, Florida, with detailed descriptions of their appearance and the circumstances of their disappearance painting a vivid picture of the case's urgency. Despite the discovery of evidence and the development of theories over the past decade, the major breakthrough needed for an arrest remains elusive. The Moriarty family, closely working with investigators, contrasts with Stacy's reported lack of engagement with the investigation. The family's enduring grief is palpable, symbolized by the urn containing Kelly's remains and their unyielding hope for justice, a sentiment poignantly echoed by Bud before his passing. The absence of closure, as Bud stated, means living with this tragedy indefinitely, with their primary aspiration being justice for the two women whose lives were so tragically cut short.

Deanne Hastings

Deanne Hastings, born on a serene winter day, February 27, 1980, in the quaint town of Pahrump, Nevada, embarked on life's journey with an exuberance that was infectious. Growing up alongside her older brother, Carson, Deanne experienced the quintessential childhood, brimming with joy and the unwavering love of her parents. Carson and Deanne were not just siblings; they were confidants, partners in crime, sharing countless hours playing under the sun-kissed skies, building castles in the sandbox, and exploring their neighborhood on their trusty bikes.

In the tapestry of her early years, a significant thread was woven when, in her fourth grade, the Hastings family uprooted their lives from the familiar terrains of Pahrump to the vibrant and verdant surroundings of Spokane, Washington. It was here that Deanne's personality blossomed like a flower in spring. Described by those who knew her as empathetic, friendly, and outgoing, Deanne was a young girl who sparkled with brilliance and fearless ambition. School became her stage, and she shone brightly, earning stellar grades and surrounding herself with a circle of friends who were drawn to her magnetic personality. Her move from Nevada to Washington only showcased her incredible adaptability and resilience.

However, the tapestry of Deanne's life began to show contrasting colors when, at the tender age of 15, the foundation of her world was shaken. Her parents, the pillars of her childhood paradise, decided to divorce, leading to her father's departure from the family home. This upheaval was compounded when Carson, her brother and childhood ally, left for a boot camp in Texas. Deanne, once the epitome of energy and joy, found herself navigating a labyrinth of change and loss, her once bright world dimming.

Despite the storms, Deanne's bond with her mother strengthened, evolving into a deep friendship. It was a partnership forged in the fires of adversity, as they supported each other through this tumultuous period. When Deanne was 17, life threw her another curveball – she discovered she was pregnant. The news filled her with a maelstrom of emotions, from trepidation to excitement. The baby's father, a high school acquaintance, joined her in this new chapter of their lives.

In July of 1998, Deanne's life was forever changed with the arrival of her son, Hayden. The young parents, fueled by love and determination, decided to cohabitate, striving to create a nurturing environment for their child. For nine years, Deanne and Hayden's father tried to weave a tapestry of family life, but despite their efforts, the relationship unraveled.

Returning to live with her mother, Deanne found herself at a crossroads. It was during this period that her behavior began to shift dramatically. Those who knew her observed episodes of intense rage and aggression, a stark contrast to the Deanne they once knew. Following these outbursts, Deanne would retreat into remorse, apologizing for her actions. However, these episodes became a recurrent, exhausting cycle, leaving her and her loved ones grappling with confusion and concern.

It was evident that something profound was affecting Deanne. After a period of struggle and introspection, she was diagnosed with bipolar disorder. This revelation shed light on her experiences but also introduced new challenges. Deanne explored various methods of self-medication, a testament to her desperate search for stability and normalcy in a world that seemed increasingly chaotic.

During this turbulent time, Hayden began living with his father, but Deanne's love and commitment as a mother never waned. She remained a constant, loving presence in his life. Seeking a fresh start, Deanne moved to Texas to live with her brother Carson, hoping that a change of scenery might offer a respite from her struggles.

In Texas, Deanne experienced a renaissance of sorts. Her mental health improved, and she rediscovered parts of herself that had been lost in the whirlwind of her life's challenges. Motivated and rejuvenated, she pursued education to become a nursing assistant, a testament to her enduring spirit and desire to help others.

It was during this period of renewal that Deanne met Randy, a friend of Carson's from boot camp. Their connection was immediate and profound, leading to a whirlwind romance that quickly blossomed into marriage. Together, they expanded their family with two more children, a son and a daughter, bringing new joy and purpose to Deanne's life.

However, life is often a tapestry of light and shadow. Despite the love and happiness that filled her days, Deanne continued to grapple with her bipolar disorder. Over the years, the challenges of managing her mental health began to resurface, casting a shadow over her marriage. After nine years, the union with Randy came to an end.

Deanne Hastings' journey, already marked by the tumultuous waves of her bipolar disorder, plunged into even deeper waters as the episodes she experienced began to exert a tremendous strain on every relationship she cherished. This added layer of adversity was yet another mountain for Deanne to climb, a challenge that tested her resilience and strength.

The situation became particularly precarious when concerns arose about Randy, her partner and a military man, potentially being deployed. This possibility loomed large over their family, as it would leave Deanne as the sole caretaker of their children. Given the escalating severity of her episodes, they collectively decided that the best course of action was for Deanne and the children to move back to Spokane, Washington, to live with her mother. However, this change of environment did not bring the solace they had hoped for. Instead, Deanne's episodes intensified, reaching levels she had never experienced before.

Realizing the gravity of her situation, Deanne made the courageous decision to seek more intensive professional help. She checked herself into an inpatient treatment facility in Idaho, entrusting her two young children to the care of her mother, Patricia. Deanne's singular focus was to reclaim her life, to find the path to wellness that would enable her to return home as the devoted mother her children deserved. Her family, buoyed by hope, supported her decision, eagerly awaiting the day she would emerge healthier and happier.

Deanne's response to the treatment was a beacon of hope. Upon completing her program, she made the wise and thoughtful decision to live independently for a period before reuniting with her mother and children. It was a time for Deanne to rediscover her autonomy, to learn the delicate balance of self-care while still maintaining the unwavering love and connection with her children, despite the physical distance.

During this period of self-discovery and gradual healing, Deanne's life took an unexpected turn. She met Mike Tibbets, and an instant spark ignited between them. Their relationship blossomed rapidly, filled with the exhilaration of new love. Deanne, brimming with happiness, often shared her joy with her brother, expressing her readiness to embark on the journey of marriage once again. Their relationship was a whirlwind of affection and hope, leading them to an engagement.

Simultaneously, Deanne felt a calling to pursue a career in cosmetology, a field where she could channel her passion for beauty and creativity. Enrolling in cosmetology school was not just a career move; it was a step towards building a life she loved, a life where she could express her artistic flair and bring joy to others.

However, life's complex tapestry brought another challenge. Deanne had to switch her bipolar medication due to changes in her insurance coverage. This critical component of her treatment plan, previously covered by her old insurance, was now inaccessible. Mike, ever supportive, offered to cover the cost out-of-pocket, but circumstances led to Deanne discontinuing her medication. This decision, though made out of necessity, posed a significant risk to her mental health.

On November 3rd, 2015, Deanne embarked on her first day at the Glen Dow Academy for cosmetology with enthusiasm and hope. Her day was filled with learning and excitement, a promising start to her new career path. That evening, she invited her son Hayden's girlfriend, Melanie, for a girls' night, a testament to her warm and nurturing nature. Despite being only 17, Deanne treated Melanie with the affection and regard of a family member.

As the night unfolded, Deanne and Melanie enjoyed each other's company, with Mike working the night shift. Melanie later recounted that Deanne was her usual happy, positive self, showing no signs of distress. After Melanie left, Deanne sent a loving text message to her, a routine gesture of care.

However, when Mike returned home later that night, he was met with an unsettling silence – Deanne was not there. A note she left indicated a quick trip to the store, but as time passed without her return, worry set in. Mike embarked on a frantic search, eventually finding Deanne's car in a public parking lot, but Deanne was nowhere to be found.

The ensuing days were a maelstrom of confusion and fear. Mike reached out to the media, hoping to find Deanne, yet, curiously, he didn't inform her family directly. This decision led to Deanne's brother, Carson, learning of her disappearance through the news – a harrowing way to discover such troubling news.

The police, informed of Deanne's mental health history, seemed less invested in her case, attributing her disappearance to her tendency to go off the grid. Despite Mike's efforts, the sense of urgency to find Deanne was dampened by this perception.

In the beginning, Carson maintained a level of calm regarding his sister Deanne's disappearance. This wasn't the first time she had vanished without a trace, so initially, he didn't panic. However, this sense of composure quickly dissolved when he spoke with their mother, Patricia. She understood that this time, the circumstances were alarmingly different.

Deanne, known for her unpredictable wanderlust, had a rule of thumb: she always informed her family before embarking on any of her impromptu adventures. It was her way of ensuring they didn't worry unnecessarily. She'd also make it a point to check in regularly, a small but comforting gesture that she was safe and sound. This time, those reassuring messages never came. Her silence was uncharacteristic and foreboding.

Four days into her disappearance, Mike, a concerned family member, decided to investigate further. He went to the trading company where Deanne's credit card had last been used on November 4th. The surveillance footage from around noon that day revealed a troubling scene. Deanne appeared at the checkout counter, her actions erratic and rushed. She seemed paranoid, constantly looking over her shoulder as if pursued by an unseen adversary. Her purchases were peculiar - energy drinks, cigarettes, birthday candles, string cheese, and vodka - items that didn't correspond with any upcoming family events or celebrations.

Witnesses from the strip mall, where the grocery store was located, painted a picture of Deanne's distressed state. A hair salon employee recalled Deanne wandering in, disoriented, referring to her as 'mommy', and sharing a harrowing tale of being drugged and kidnapped. Others observed her sitting outside the mall, appearing disheveled and agitated. When concerned passersby offered assistance, she became confrontational.

The situation escalated when police and EMTs arrived for a wellness check. Deanne was uncooperative and confrontational, refusing to provide her name and insisting she had been drugged and assaulted. However, the responding officer perceived her as merely intoxicated and, finding no evidence of physical abuse, did not pursue the matter further. This decision later became a contentious point, given Deanne's apparent distressed state.

As days passed, the family intensified their search efforts, distributing flyers across the city. It wasn't until November 7th, five days after Deanne's last sighting, that Mike received a crucial lead. An employee from the grocery store claimed to have spent time with Deanne the night before her disappearance. This encounter, initially perceived as innocuous, took a sinister turn when inconsistencies emerged in the employee's recounting of the events. He altered his story, admitting to drinking and smoking marijuana with Deanne, raising suspicions about his involvement in her disappearance.

Further investigation into Deanne's car, which was found with her personal belongings but missing some credit cards, led nowhere. Attempts to trace her movements through credit card transactions uncovered more disturbing details. Surveillance footage from various locations showed a man, identified as Randy Riley, using Deanne's credit card. This revelation, combined with witness sightings of Deanne in a visibly distressed state in the company of Riley and others, painted a troubling picture of her last known activities.

The police, piecing together these fragmented clues, constructed a timeline tracing Deanne's movements from the grocery store to a storage facility and eventually to Riley's apartment. Despite her visible distress, witnesses who encountered her attributed her condition to emotional turmoil from a supposed divorce, failing to recognize the gravity of her situation.

In a captivating turn of events, police officers interrogated a man named Randy, unraveling a mysterious and intricate tale. Randy recounted an evening where he, along with his friend James, encountered Dan near a storage unit. The trio spent time together, indulging in drinks and camaraderie. Amidst this seemingly casual gathering, Randy claimed that Dan, in a surprising gesture, handed over her credit cards to him, insisting he treat himself to a meal. This part of Randy's account, however, raised suspicions among the police. They found it hard to believe that Dan would so casually entrust her credit cards to someone else. Doubting the credibility of his story, the police apprehended Randy on charges of second-degree identity theft and subjected him to further interrogation.

As the questioning deepened, Randy's narrative took a perplexing turn. He painted a picture of a challenging time in his life, having been evicted from his apartment and resorting to using a storage facility. It was here, he said, that he and James came across Dan, who appeared intoxicated and belligerent. Despite her state, Randy and James decided to spend a couple of hours with her. Randy's description of the night's events continued with an odd incident. He claimed that during their walk down South Inland Empire Way, Dan needed to use the restroom and ventured into some bushes up a hill. Intriguingly, Randy stated that James went to check on her, after which Dan supposedly emerged and parted ways with them. The last he saw of her was on the side of the road, and upon returning the next day, he stumbled upon her abandoned shoes and coat, discovering her credit cards in the pockets.

The circumstances grew more peculiar as Randy noted the time of year – mid-November in Washington – making Dan's decision to discard her shoes and jacket in the cold weather seem illogical and suspicious. Meanwhile, police had found Dan's license in downtown Spokane, which Randy later admitted to discarding there in an attempt to mislead the investigation. He also confessed to disposing of her jacket and shoes but maintained ignorance regarding her whereabouts.

Randy's arrest and a 13-month sentence for identity theft was not the end of the investigation. The police turned their attention to James, seeking his version of events. James contradicted Randy's story, claiming ignorance of the theft and offering a different account of the night Dan disappeared. He suggested it was Randy, not himself, who had gone up the hill to check on Dan. According to James, Randy returned alone, saying Dan chose to stay in the bushes. The inconsistencies in their stories perplexed the investigators.

The location of these events, just 300 yards from Dan's home, prompted an extensive search involving sniffer dogs, helicopters, and foot patrols, but Dan remained elusive. The investigation then shifted to Mike Tibbets, Dan's fiancé, amidst mixed accounts of their relationship's stability. Text messages and testimonies from Dan's close acquaintances hinted at potential turmoil and unsettling accusations from Dan towards Mike.

The case took another twist when Amanda, Dan's best friend, received a frantic Facebook message from James, claiming urgent information for Dan's family. However, when confronted, James backtracked, offering no new insights, leaving the family and investigators in a state of frustration and uncertainty.

In the quaint town where everyone knew each other's stories, Amanda rallied a remarkable search party, reminiscent of a close-knit community coming together in times of crisis. This search wasn't just a routine effort; it was a poignant reminder of the bonds formed in high school, now reignited in a desperate quest to find Deanne. Amanda's call to action resonated deeply, bringing together old friends, former classmates, and a host of volunteers, all united by a single purpose: to uncover the truth about Deanne's mysterious disappearance.

This wasn't just any day; it was Dan Hastings' 36th birthday, a day that should have been filled with celebration and joy. Instead, it was marked by an intense, coordinated search, with emotions running high. The search teams, now divided into eight diligent groups, set out to scour various locations where

Deanne was last seen. The air was thick with a mix of hope and anxiety as these teams ventured into the unknown, driven by the shared belief that more eyes and more hearts searching meant a better chance of finding Deanne.

The community's response was overwhelming, a testament to the impact Deanne had on those around her. People from all walks of life showed up, each carrying a glimmer of hope that their efforts would shed light on Deanne's whereabouts. This collective effort was a powerful expression of community spirit, with everyone clinging to the hope of new information, however small.

As the volunteers meticulously retraced Deanne's last known steps, they grappled with a mix of emotions. There was the intense desire to know what happened, the desperate hope to find her safe, and the lingering fear of the unknown. Every participant shared a common wish: for Deanne to reach out, to let someone know she was okay. Such a simple act would bring immense relief to so many hearts.

Yet, despite these tireless efforts, the mystery deepened. No new evidence surfaced, no sightings, no leads. The case of Dan Hastings seemed to hit a dead end, leaving everyone involved with more questions than answers. The community was left in a state of limbo, holding onto hope against the odds.

Theories began to circulate, each trying to make sense of the baffling situation. One prevailing theory suggested that Deanne, known to have struggled with mental health issues, might have wandered off during a manic episode. This theory was bolstered by her recent discontinuation of medication, which might have exacerbated her symptoms. People remembered how Deanne used to inform others before going off-grid during her episodes, but this time, perhaps things were different. The theory postulated that her mental state might have prevented her from reaching out, or worse, made her believe that those closest to her posed a threat.

As people pieced together her last known movements, including her erratic behavior and incoherent speech, the possibility of Deanne wandering off into oblivion seemed increasingly plausible. Could she have become so disoriented that she lost all sense of identity, perhaps even joining the ranks of the homeless, unseen and unrecognized?

Yet, doubts lingered. If Deanne had indeed wandered off, wouldn't someone have seen her? The lack of sightings post-Randy encounter was puzzling. And then there were the questions about the longevity of her manic state – could it really last for years without respite?

Another theory, equally grim, suggested that Deanne might have succumbed to the elements or other hazards after wandering off. The discovery of her jacket and shoes lent some credence to this idea. However, like the first theory, it too was fraught with uncertainties. The extensive search efforts seemed to contradict the idea that she could have perished nearby without being found.

The first theory revolves around the perplexing actions of the employee at the trading company, a grocery store. This individual's encounter with Deanne outside the Knitting Factory, leading to a night of drinking and smoking at his place, raises numerous questions. His ambiguous recognition of Deanne when confronted with a missing person's flyer, followed by his sudden relocation to Florida, strikes as peculiar and untimely. While his explanation of financial constraints seems plausible, the coincidence of his departure cannot be ignored. Yet, despite these oddities, his account does align with other sightings of Deanne, suggesting that she might have independently left his vicinity.

Next, the spotlight turns to Mike Tibbets, Deanne's fiancé, whose actions in the wake of her disappearance are shrouded in ambiguity. His delayed report to the police, coupled with his seemingly passive response to her missing status, including his handling of her car and possessions, raises eyebrows. While some may view these as signs of guilt or concealment, another perspective considers the possibility of a man overwhelmed by the situation, perhaps accustomed to Deanne's sporadic disappearances due to her mental health struggles. His reluctance to part with her last belongings could be seen as a clinging to memories, rather than a calculated effort to obstruct justice.

Finally, the most compelling theory implicates Randy Riley and his friend James. Their last known interaction with Deanne, coupled with Randy's suspicious use of her credit cards and inconsistent stories, paints a picture of potential foul play. James's erratic behavior, hinting at guilt yet withholding information, further deepens the mystery. The theory posits that they might have seen Deanne as an easy target due to her vulnerable state, leading to a tragic outcome. Randy's return to the scene and his inexplicable acquisition of Deanne's belongings could indicate a desperate attempt to cover up a heinous act.

Each theory weaves a complex web of possibilities, leaving more questions than answers. The true fate of Deanne remains shrouded in mystery, a heartbreaking puzzle yet to be solved. The lingering doubts and contrasting hypotheses underscore the tragic reality that, in cases like Deanne's, the truth is often elusive, leaving loved ones and investigators grappling with the unbearable weight of the unknown.

Branson Perry

The story of Branson Perry is both haunting and deeply human, a narrative that resonates with the fragility and complexity of life. At the young age of 20, Branson's disappearance casts a shadow over the seemingly mundane tapestry of his life, a life that, while unremarkable in the grand scheme, was uniquely his own. This isn't meant to diminish his existence; rather, it highlights the fact that Branson was much like any other young person, living a life filled with both promise and ordinary struggles.

Hailing from the heartland of America, Branson grew up in Middle America's quintessential small town, Skidmore. He was a proud graduate of Nodaway Holt High School, class of 1999. After graduation, Branson's journey was not one of immediate success or clear direction. He moved through various jobs, a reflection not so much of his work ethic, which was commendable, but more so of the limited opportunities in a small town like Skidmore.

Those who knew Branson saw him as a good kid. He earned money mainly through roofing, a job demanding both physical strength and resilience. When roofing work was scarce, Branson didn't sit idle; he found work assisting with a traveling petting zoo, demonstrating his adaptability and willingness to take on whatever work came his way.

Branson's life, however, wasn't all work and no play. In his free time, he dedicated himself to martial arts, earning a black belt in Hapkido, a remarkable achievement especially considering he suffered from tachycardia, a condition that causes an abnormally fast heart rate. Physically, Branson was a striking figure: tall at 6 feet, with a lean frame, short blonde hair, and a smile that was both welcoming and memorable.

His interests were typical of many young men of his age – a love for sports, music, and enjoying time with friends. Branson's family life was shaped by his parents' divorce. While his mother remained an important part of his life, he lived with his father, Bob, in a modest, single-story home at 304 West Oak Street in Skidmore. This home, like many in the town, reflected the unassuming lifestyle of its residents.

But the essence of a person is often more than what's visible on the surface. Obituaries might list the facts of a life, but they seldom capture the soul of the person. In the days leading up to Branson's mysterious disappearance, an encounter with Jason Beerman, a neighbor, emerged as potentially significant. Jason, who was somewhat older and had a reputation for being a bit sketchy, was friendly enough with Branson for the two to spend time together.

On April 7th, four days before Branson vanished, the two were together at Jason's house. In an effort to alleviate the boredom that can often permeate small-town life, Jason allegedly gave Branson an unidentified drug. The effects of this drug were dramatic, leading to behavior that was out of character for Branson. According to Diane Fanning, a true crime investigator who delved deeply into this case, Branson's actions that day were erratic and alarming.

Many people who knew Branson had long suspected that he might be gay, a suspicion shared by his father, Bob. However, Branson never openly acknowledged his sexuality. The reasons for his silence on this matter are his own, but it is possible that this internal conflict contributed to his decision to experiment with drugs.

April 8th was a day much like any other for Branson, marked by a routine visit to the hospital where his father, Bob, was recovering from an illness and recent surgery. These visits had become a staple of Branson's daily life, a testament to the bond between father and son. During these moments of quiet hospital room conversation, Branson confided in his father about the unsettling events that had transpired at their neighbor's house.

Bob's reaction to his son's revelation was a visceral blend of anger and protective paternal instinct. To him, Branson was more than just a young adult; he was his child, his boy, whose wellbeing was paramount. The thought that their neighbor, Jason, might have drugged and taken advantage of Branson ignited a fury within Bob. He was incensed, feeling a deep urge to confront Jason. However, his own health constraints, confined as he was to the hospital bed, made this impossible. This confrontation, a moment of potential catharsis and truth-seeking, would never occur. By the time Bob was discharged from the hospital, his son had vanished, turning his focus to a far more dire situation.

The timing of Branson's disappearance, coming just days after this disturbing incident, painted a picture riddled with questions and haunting possibilities. While Jason was never officially named as a suspect, he was questioned by authorities. This led many to ponder if there was more to the story, more to that day's events that had yet to surface. Was it possible that Jason, fearing repercussions for his actions, had taken drastic measures? Or did the drug that Branson allegedly took have lingering effects, altering his state of mind or decision-making in a way that directly influenced his disappearance?

On that fateful Wednesday, April 11th, 2001, the day unfolded with a sense of normalcy that belied the extraordinary events about to unfold. Branson Perry, a young man known for his willingness to lend a hand, was engaged in a thorough cleaning of his father's house. This was not just any routine clean-up; it was a special effort to welcome his dad home from the hospital. To assist him in this endeavor, he called upon his close friend Jenna Crawford, who eagerly joined in to help tidy up the family abode.

Meanwhile, the family car, a steadfast but weary vehicle, sat in the driveway, in desperate need of a new alternator. To address this, Branson had arranged for two mechanics to come by and work on the car. They busied themselves with the task at hand, their tools clinking and clattering as they worked diligently outside.

Inside, Branson and Jenna were a whirlwind of activity – vacuuming carpets, polishing windows, and diligently wiping down countertops. It was during these mundane tasks that a seemingly insignificant moment caught Jenna's attention. She noticed Branson hastily grabbing something from the kitchen cabinet and darting outside. The action was brief and seemingly inconsequential, but in light of the events that were to unfold, it would later take on a much more ominous significance. Jenna couldn't help but wonder, in retrospect, what Branson had taken from the cabinet, and for what purpose.

After completing the chores, Jenna took a well-deserved shower, emerging refreshed and ready for a drink. It was then that she encountered one of the mechanics inside the house, rummaging through the very cabinets Branson had accessed earlier. His presence inside startled her, and she inquired about what he was searching for. His response was vague, offering nothing but a brief dismissal before he returned outside. This interaction, though brief, would later resonate with a sense of foreboding.

As the day waned, Jenna went upstairs to rest. It was then that she saw Branson outside on the front lawn. She called out to him, inquiring about his plans. His response was casual yet definitive, "I'm going to put away the jumper cables and then run out for a bit. I'll be back in a few minutes." Those words, seemingly ordinary at the time, would echo in the minds of all who knew him.

It was approximately 3:00 p.m. when Jenna last saw Branson Perry, a detail she would recall with unsettling clarity. Branson appeared to be heading towards the shed on the property, a likely destination given it housed the jumper cables and other tools. However, beyond this point, the narrative of Branson's day becomes shrouded in mystery. No one, not Jenna, the two mechanics working on the car, nor any of the neighbors, witnessed him actually leaving the property. The destination he had in mind remains unknown, as Branson had not shared his plans with anyone.

Compounding the mystery, Branson left behind several personal items: his wallet, keys, and a paycheck he had recently cashed. These belongings suggested an intent to return shortly, a detail that would later fuel much speculation about the nature of his disappearance. Jenna, assuming nothing amiss, eventually departed from the house, believing that Branson had perhaps become sidetracked. The mechanics, too, wrapped up their work and left, unaware of the gravity of the situation that was slowly unfolding.

It was Branson's grandmother, Joanne Stinnet, who first sensed that something was amiss. When she visited her son, Bob, in the hospital the following day, she inquired about Branson. Bob's response was concerning: he had not seen Branson the day before, nor had he heard from him at all. This was particularly unusual since Branson had been a constant presence at the hospital, visiting his father daily without fail.

With a growing sense of unease, Joanne stopped by the Perry residence on her way home. She was met with an unsettling scene: the front door was unlocked, yet there was no sign of Branson inside. She waited for hours, hoping for his return, and made several calls to his friends to ascertain his whereabouts, but to no avail. The lack of any word from Branson was out of character and alarming, especially to a family that was closely knit.

As night fell and Branson remained unaccounted for, Joanne's concern escalated into action. She made the decisive call to the police, initiating what would become a frantic and extensive search.

The search for Branson Perry evolved into a vast and intricate operation, drawing in various law enforcement agencies including local police, the

Missouri State Highway Patrol, and a host of volunteers. Aerial and ground searches scoured the area, extending to fields and woodlands within a 15-mile radius. As the search intensified, a different picture of Branson began to emerge, one that even those closest to him hadn't fully seen.

It was uncovered that Branson had been grappling with a hidden drug addiction, a struggle he had kept concealed even from his family and close friends. Despite this, he had been planning to go to rehab, hoping to reclaim control over his life. This revelation offered a new perspective on why Branson had confided in his father about the incident at his neighbor's house. At 20 years old, Branson was legally an adult, but his father's anger stemmed not just from the possibility that his son was taken advantage of by the neighbor, Jason, but also from the frustration that Jason was fueling Branson's drug problem at a time when he was trying to break free from it.

With Branson's past with drugs coming to light and considering his personal belongings and cash were left behind, authorities began to suspect foul play. They theorized that what Branson hastily grabbed from the cabinet could have been drugs, possibly his own stash that he intended to sell before heading off to rehab. The identity of the person he might have met that day, they speculated, could hold the key to understanding what happened to him.

As months passed, the case took a bizarre and unexpected turn. Hundreds of people were interviewed, including Branson's friends known to be involved in drugs, but all leads seemed to lead nowhere. Lie detector tests were administered to individuals last known to have seen Branson, including the mechanics at his house, his friend Jenna, and the neighbor Jason. Remarkably, all passed the tests, deepening the enigma surrounding Branson's disappearance.

The case eventually went cold, but on the eve of its two-year anniversary, a chilling development arose. On April 10th, 2003, 59-year-old Jack Rogers was arrested on charges unrelated to Branson's case. Rogers, outwardly a respected member of society, a Presbyterian Church minister, and a Boy Scout leader, was apprehended for first-degree assault and practicing medicine without a license, related to a makeshift gender reassignment surgery in a hotel room in Columbia, Missouri.

The investigation into Rogers revealed a dark and twisted side. Police, while searching his property and computer, found disturbing images of young people and evidence of Rogers' participation in graphic online forums under pseudonyms like "buggerbud" and "extreme body mods." His posts detailed gruesome acts of mutilation that he claimed to have personally conducted. Rogers became a person of interest in Branson's case due to his proximity to Skidmore and a story he recounted online about picking up a young blonde hitchhiker, whom he claimed to have tortured, mutilated, and murdered, before burying the body in the Ozarks.

Among Rogers' possessions, police discovered a turtle claw necklace resembling one Branson owned. Despite these unsettling findings, Rogers denied any involvement in Branson's disappearance, insisting that his online writings were purely fictional. At his sentencing for the other crimes, Branson's mother pleaded with Rogers to disclose any information about her son. Rogers maintained his innocence in Branson's case, leaving her and the authorities without definitive answers.

The absence of Branson's body has made it nearly impossible to conclusively link anyone to the crime. The prevailing belief, however, is that Branson is no longer alive, a tragic conclusion to a case that began as a simple missing person investigation and spiraled into a tale of deep mystery and dark secrets.

Jeremy Alex

Born and raised in the quaint, coastal town of Belfast, Maine, Jeremy's early years were split between living with his mother, Paula Caswell, during the school year, and spending his sun-drenched summers in Portsmouth, New Hampshire, under the loving care of his father, Ted, and stepmother, Susan Alex. Their lives intertwined when Jeremy was merely six, marking the beginning of a bond that grew stronger with time. Despite the initial turmoil of his parents' divorce, Jeremy formed a close and affectionate relationship with his stepmother. Susan, in her heartfelt recollections, expressed how Jeremy became as dear to her as a biological son.

Belfast, where Jeremy spent most of his formative years, was a picturesque small town, nestled on the coast with lush forests and majestic mountains in close proximity. This close-knit community, characterized by its sole stoplight, thrived on the ebb and flow of seacoast tourism, which brought a variety of people into Jeremy's life. The town's natural beauty and the ever-changing faces of tourists fostered in Jeremy a profound appreciation for the great outdoors. He relished activities like hiking, snowboarding, and swimming, making full use of the diverse terrains that surrounded him. His athleticism wasn't confined to outdoor pursuits alone; he was also an active participant in little league during his youth, always seeking opportunities to immerse himself in nature. Susan fondly recalled how Jeremy embraced a minimalist lifestyle, a reflection of Belfast's ethos, where simplicity and a deep connection with nature were the norm.

As Jeremy navigated his teenage years, he exhibited a streak of rebellion, a phase that is often a rite of passage into adulthood. However, he eventually mellowed, becoming more grounded and family-oriented as he stepped into his twenties. His passion for music, particularly his admiration for the Grateful Dead, played a pivotal role in his journey post-high school graduation. For two years, Jeremy embarked on an adventurous chapter of his life, following the Grateful Dead around the country. He embraced a nomadic lifestyle, living out of a van and sustaining himself by selling grilled cheese sandwiches - a testament to his resourceful and free-spirited nature.

As time went on, Jeremy's bond with his family, including his parents and stepmother, deepened significantly. The rebellious distance of his younger years gave way to a dedicated and loving relationship with his family. He never missed an opportunity to connect with them on birthdays and holidays, regardless of his whereabouts in the country. Susan affectionately described Jeremy's approach to life as one where he 'worked to live, not lived to work.' His career path was unconventional; he wasn't tethered to a stable job but instead took on various odd jobs and seasonal work, sometimes venturing out of state. His stint with Greenpeace in California, along with his skills in landscaping and gardening, highlighted his adaptability and love for the outdoors. Jeremy's proficiency in home improvement and house painting further exemplified his versatile skill set, which allowed him the freedom to travel and explore different places. Susan reminisced about Jeremy's simplicity and contentment with life, how he didn't require much to be happy, and his innate love for reading and gardening.

When Jeremy was 24, he met Suzanne Forkeran, affectionately known as Susie, through mutual friends. Their connection was instant and profound, with Susie later reflecting on the strong, almost predestined draw she felt towards him. This magnetic personality of Jeremy was something his friends, like Kathy Langlier, also echoed. Kathy, who shared a love for the Grateful Dead with Jeremy, described him as a welcoming, kind presence who was easy to be around. She had been a long-standing friend of Jeremy and was thrilled when he and Susie started their relationship. Kathy observed how their relationship blossomed from a solid foundation of friendship, calling it a 'beautiful evolution.'

Susie moved to New York to be with Jeremy, however, their journey took a challenging turn when they decided to move back to Belfast, a decision that marked the beginning of a difficult period in their relationship.

Initially, Jeremy was a picture of sobriety, steering clear of alcohol and cigarettes, though he did occasionally indulge in marijuana. This was a stark contrast to his later years in Belfast, where he gradually found himself entangled in the darker aspects of rural life, experimenting with harder substances like cocaine and heroin. This shift in Jeremy's behavior was subtle at first, manifesting in infrequent weekend binges that gradually became more frequent and intense.

Susie, though deeply concerned, tried to maintain a boundary, urging Jeremy to keep his substance use away from her. As spring arrived, Jeremy's behavior became increasingly erratic, his use of drugs more frequent, leading to noticeable changes in his demeanor. Friends, including Kathy, observed that Jeremy seemed paranoid, a stark departure from his usual self. However, even amidst this turmoil, there were glimmers of hope and normalcy. Jeremy spoke of buying land in Belfast and settling down, a dream that seemed to temporarily anchor him back to his aspirations and the life he shared with Susie.

Their relationship, though strained, still had moments of joy and togetherness. One such day was April 22nd, when the couple enjoyed a trip to Sugarloaf for snowboarding. Yet, the return home that evening seemed to reignite Jeremy's inner turmoil. He abruptly left for their new house in Northport, a move that Susie suspected was driven by his desire to use drugs.

The following days were a whirlwind of confusion and concern. A friend of

Jeremy's revealed that they had spent a night indulging in cocaine and heroin at the Northport house. Back in Portsmouth, Jeremy's parents, unaware of his struggles, planned a visit, oblivious to the storm brewing in their son's life.

On April 24th, Jeremy's behavior took a worrying turn. He returned to Susie, agitated and delusional, accusing her and friends of bizarre conspiracies. This confrontation left Susie distraught, but she hoped Jeremy would find some peace and clarity after some rest. However, when she tried to reconnect with him shortly after, she found him distant and unwilling to open up.

Jeremy left around 11 am, marking the beginning of a series of events that would add to the mystery surrounding his actions. Later that day, he was seen in a state of distress by Cynthia Munkelt and her husband James. Recognized by Cynthia, a teacher at Belfast Area High School, Jeremy exhibited signs of paranoia and hallucination, speaking of being pursued by unspecified 'bad guys.' Despite the couple's efforts to calm him, the sound of approaching sirens triggered Jeremy to flee into the woods, leaving behind a trail of confusion and concern.

This incident was followed by another sighting of Jeremy crossing a nearby highway, and then disappearing into the woods behind a local business. This was the last confirmed sighting of Jeremy Alex.

The local police, fire department, and ambulance services sprung into action upon receiving a distressing call but were met with an eerie silence as they found no trace of Jeremy. Undeterred, they resumed their efforts the following day, the 25th, leading to a startling discovery: Jeremy's van, desolate and abandoned, on a secluded gravel road amidst land owned by the Humane Society. The scene was unsettling, with the van located off of Pound Hill Road, Jeremy's phone and keys ominously left behind, hinting at an abrupt and mysterious departure.

The police delved into the contents of Jeremy's phone, uncovering vital information that led them to immediately contact his father, Ted. However, the news would not reach Ted until the next morning, as he had not heard the message until then. The police conveyed to him that they were earnestly searching for Jeremy and had found his car and belongings in an abandoned state.

Susan, grappling with the shock and disbelief of the situation, reflected on her initial thoughts, emphasizing the unsettling nature of the circumstances. Despite the shock, there wasn't an immediate fear of something horrific, but rather a sense of something being amiss. With urgency, Ted and Susan embarked on a journey to Belfast, hoping for answers. En route, Susan reached out to Susie around 7 am, sharing the distressing news of Jeremy's van and phone being found, and his unexplained absence, but was met with the frustrating reality of limited information from the authorities.

Susie, taking matters into her own hands, decided to first visit the house in Northport before approaching the police. The house held clues that Jeremy had returned there, as furniture he had taken earlier was inside. However, a sense of alarm grew as she discovered the door ajar, keys still in the lock, and the house in disarray, signaling that Jeremy might have been in a troubled state. The discovery of cocaine and heroin, which she promptly disposed of, only added to the mounting concerns.

Upon the arrival of Susan and Ted, Susie had already mobilized a few of Jeremy's friends for an impromptu search, as formal authorities were still organizing their resources. The search was a race against time, with the harsh cold of April in Maine presenting a daunting challenge for anyone lost in the wilderness. Suzy commented on the treacherous nature of the Maine woods, comparing it to a perilous journey rather than a simple walk in the park.

The search escalated on the 26th with the involvement of the Waldo County Sheriff's Department and the Maine Wardens Service, bringing expertise in search and rescue operations. The search was meticulous, involving tracking dogs, search and rescue officers, and volunteers, all equipped with tracking devices to ensure no area was overlooked. Despite their best efforts, including the deployment of ultralight aircraft, no trace of Jeremy was found.

As the days passed, hope began to wane. The police officially called off the search on April 27th. However, Ted and a group of volunteers, driven by determination and love, continued their search. Ted even chartered a private plane to scour the area from above. Susan, in the meantime, sought answers from Jeremy's friends, imploring them to reveal any information they might have, emphasizing the critical nature of the situation.

Ted, Susan, and their friend Neil Ouellette persisted in urging the authorities to resume the search, holding onto hope that Jeremy, with his outdoor skills and resourcefulness, could still be alive. Kathy, sharing in this belief, expressed confidence in Jeremy's survival abilities. However, as time ticked on, the reality of the situation began to sink in, with Ted acknowledging the grim likelihood of Jeremy not being alive if he was still in the woods.

In a desperate bid to find Jeremy, Ted and Susan turned to the media on April 29th. Ted's position as the president of the Portsmouth Rotary Club, an organization known for its influential and affluent members, lent weight to their appeals. The media took up the story, spurred by Ted's prominent status in the community. Additionally, the family enlisted the help of Shamshack Investigative Services, a private investigation firm, to further amplify their efforts in the media, including coverage by the Portsmouth Herald.

Although they resided in New Hampshire, Ted and his family garnered attention in Ted's town in New Hampshire, as well as from the local Bangor Daily News in Maine, for their efforts to raise awareness about Jeremy's disappearance. On April 29th, Ted informed the Bangor Daily News that Jeremy had no known history of drug use or mental health issues that could account for his hallucinations. Despite being unaware of the underlying problems leading up to Jeremy's disappearance, the family remained hopeful.

Portsmouth's Mayor, Evelyn Cyril, publicly expressed her support for the family, emphasizing the profound impact such incidents have on parents. Bob Keating, Chief Deputy at the Waldo County Sheriff's Office, acknowledged the fruitless results of the initial search efforts but remained optimistic.

A sighting reported on Route 1 refocused the search efforts, and a subsequent search on May 2nd covered both the woods along Route 1 and expanded into the Belfast area. Despite extensive efforts involving Maine Wardens and search dogs, no trace of Jeremy was found. Keating mentioned that they were still pursuing leads and conducting follow-up interviews.

Initially, Jeremy's friends were not very forthcoming, and the situation appeared bleak. However, once Jeremy's drug use was disclosed by Susie, who had initially concealed this information to avoid legal repercussions for Jeremy, the police's focus shifted to investigating the drug angle. This change led to even less cooperation from Jeremy's friends.

Further developments in the case included a motorist's report of seeing someone resembling Jeremy talking to two men in a red pickup truck in an area known for drug activity. This sighting fueled speculations of foul play.

Despite exhaustive searches, including a large-scale search on September 24th involving various groups and covering an expanded area, no significant leads were found. A mistaken identity incident in Owls Head, involving another individual named Jeremy, briefly reignited hopes but ultimately led nowhere.

Frustrated with the lack of progress, Ted urged state police to treat Jeremy's disappearance as a homicide investigation. Meanwhile, Ted and Susan continued their own efforts, examining maps, posting reward posters, and following up on various tips suggesting foul play.

Ted's unwavering hope and enduring efforts to keep Jeremy's memory alive transformed a deeply personal tragedy into a beacon of positivity for others.

The celebration in honor of Jeremy was not just a somber remembrance but a vivid tapestry of his life, painted through heartfelt stories shared by those who knew him best. His girlfriend Susie, friends from Maine, and his family all found solace in recalling his vibrant spirit and his profound love for the outdoors, music, and the adventures he embarked on while following the Grateful Dead. Jeremy was fondly remembered as a free spirit with a carefree lifestyle, a depiction that brought both smiles and tears to those gathered.

In April 2005, Ted's initiative to start the Jeremy Alex Fund was a monumental step towards transforming grief into action. The fund aimed to support at-risk youth in the Seacoast area, embodying Ted's desire to forge a positive outcome from the heartbreak of his son's disappearance. Remarkably, the fund quickly garnered $32,000 in just its first week, a testament to the community's support and the impact Jeremy's story had on people.

The subsequent years saw Ted and Jeremy's sister Paula Caswell embarking on an awareness tour for missing people. This journey, tracing the route of Leah Roberts who vanished in 2000, not only raised awareness but also connected them with others sharing similar sorrows. Paula's determination to find Jeremy was palpable as she painstakingly entered his information into every missing person's database available, a relentless quest for answers.

During one poignant stop in Kentucky, Paula's heartfelt speech revealed her daily struggle with hope and despair. She shared how Jeremy's absence affected their daily lives, yet underscored his enduring presence in their hearts. Jeremy, described as smart, caring, and kind-hearted, had left an indelible mark on those who knew him.

The search for answers took a dramatic turn in August when a woman's claim led police to search Knight's Pond in Northport for Jeremy's body. Despite the search yielding no results, it underscored the ongoing mystery surrounding his disappearance.

On the three-year anniversary of Jeremy's disappearance, Ted spoke about the state police taking over the investigation. The shift from a missing person to a homicide investigation, due to possible drug connections, added a grim dimension to the narrative. Despite the lack of concrete findings, Ted expressed satisfaction with the investigation's progress, clinging to the hope that someday the truth would surface.

Ted's revelation about Jeremy's involvement in the drug scene was a difficult acknowledgment. He speculated that Jeremy's connections might have played a role in his disappearance, a thought that haunted him.

The Jeremy Alex Fund continued to grow, raising an impressive $200,000 by December 2007. This fund's impact was evident in numerous initiatives, like providing chess sets to local fourth graders and sponsoring a student's life-changing trip to Costa Rica. These acts of kindness were not just charitable deeds but also a way for Ted to channel his grief into helping others.

In August 2008, an unexpected email from retired highway patrol officer Jim Baker brought a new twist to the case. Baker had found Jeremy's license and some money, which had been kept as beachside finds by his friend Tim Dougal. This discovery rekindled hope and prompted Ted to search the Maine beaches, though the delay in reporting the find meant potential clues had been lost to time.

Six years into his son's disappearance, Ted's reflections in a 2010 interview with the Waldo Village Soup were poignant. He spoke about the difficult journey of hope, acceptance, and the shift to focusing on positive actions. His conviction that someone out there held the key to solving the mystery of Jeremy's disappearance remained strong. Despite his belief that Jeremy was likely no longer alive, Ted's determination to uncover the truth and possibly prevent other families from experiencing similar pain was undiminished.

In 2011, the case was brought into the spotlight by the Investigation Discovery show "Disappeared". The executive producer, Elizabeth Fisher, conveyed that the case resonated deeply with those working on the episode, largely due to the profound impact Jeremy had on those who knew him. He wasn't just a fleeting acquaintance in people's lives; he was someone who left a lasting impression, deeply affecting both his family and friends.

This particular episode of "Disappeared" clarified numerous aspects of the case and delved into the widely discussed sighting in Owl's Head. The sighting had been somewhat misinterpreted in the missing person's database, The Charlie Project, which suggested these sightings might have been of Jeremy Alex. This discrepancy raised concerns, as it potentially indicated that Jeremy might have been lost in the woods or was possibly still living there, a notion that seemed to contradict other evidence.

The show also served as a primary source for quotes from Susie, Jeremy's girlfriend, as she had not been extensively interviewed by newspapers. Through this episode, viewers gained insight into her thoughts and feelings, as well as those of Susan, Jeremy's stepmother. The narrative explored how Jeremy's loved ones were coping and moving forward, despite the lingering mystery of his disappearance.

Ted and Susan, though no longer together, continued to collaborate whenever new information surfaced, although such instances were rare. Susan remained convinced that Jeremy's friends knew more about his disappearance than they were letting on, but efforts to get them to open up were met with little cooperation.

In a poignant reflection of time's passage, the house that Jeremy and Susie had planned to move into now stood abandoned. Over a year after Jeremy's disappearance, Susie moved back to California, but she kept a living connection to Jeremy through Gonzo, the dog they had chosen together. She affectionately noted similarities between Gonzo's feisty character and Jeremy's own spirited nature.

Ted, channeling his grief into positive action, continued to be actively involved with the Jeremy Alex Fund. He frequently visited schools benefiting from the fund, sharing stories about Jeremy in a manner suitable for young children. By 2011, the fund had achieved the remarkable feat of providing chess sets to 800 fourth graders in the local Seacoast area.

The "Disappeared" episode also explored various theories about what might have happened to Jeremy. Susan speculated that Jeremy might not be in the woods but rather in the ocean, considering the bay's currents. Local fishermen and boat captains seemed to agree with this assessment, suggesting that a body could be quickly dragged out to sea by the currents.

Susie, reflecting on Jeremy's drug use, pondered whether his fears of being pursued were drug-induced hallucinations or based on real threats. She recalled Jeremy mentioning these fears not only to her but also to others, including the couple who tried to assist him, suggesting there might have been some truth to his claims.

Ted, speaking with the Bangor Daily News, shared his personal belief that Jeremy was a victim of foul play. This theory, rooted in the various strange circumstances surrounding Jeremy's disappearance, painted a grim picture of what might have befallen him. Despite the passage of time, the mystery of Jeremy Alex's disappearance continued to haunt those who knew him, leaving them with more questions than answers.

Bianca Lebron

On a crisp autumn morning, the air tinged with the scent of falling leaves, ten-year-old Bianca Lebron made her way to Elias Howe School, a place she adored. This brick edifice, a familiar sight in her young life, was where she delved into the wonders of fifth grade. For Bianca, school was more than just a place of learning; it was a realm where friendships blossomed and daily adventures unfolded. Unlike some of her peers, she never sought reasons to escape its walls, never feigned illness, nor expressed disinterest in attending. School, for her, was a source of joy and excitement, a place she looked forward to visiting each day.

However, on the morning of November 7, 2001, Bianca's routine took an unexpected turn. Her eyes sparkled with a different kind of excitement, unrelated to the usual academic pursuits or the prospect of spending time with friends. That day, Bianca shared with her classmates and teacher a special plan: she would not be attending classes. Instead, she was poised for a thrilling excursion - a shopping spree with her uncle. The allure of a day filled with the joys of picking out new clothes or toys is something few children would pass up, and Bianca was no exception.

Witnesses recall Bianca's cheerful discussion with her teacher, confidently stating that her uncle would be picking her up for the day. To her friends, she painted a vivid picture of a shopping adventure at the mall, even generously extending an invitation to join her. It was a gesture that spoke volumes about her kind and inclusive nature. None of her friends took up the offer, but they likely envied her fortunate turn of events. Remarkably, no one questioned the authenticity of her plans; no signed parental note was sought, nor any verification calls made. The school simply accepted her word.

As the school day commenced, a two-tone brown van, a bit aged in appearance, pulled up in front of the school. Bianca, with a skip in her step, moved towards the van, away from the school and her classmates. The door swung open, and she hopped in, greeted by a man described by onlookers as an older Hispanic male in his late twenties or early thirties, dark-haired and bearded. The man's presence raised no suspicions; to all who saw, he was simply Bianca's uncle, there to whisk her away on her promised adventure. As the van drove off, Bianca's teacher marked her absent, unaware of the dire implications of this seemingly ordinary event.

The heart-wrenching truth, however, was that Bianca Lebron had no uncle, and her family had no knowledge of this supposed shopping trip. They believed her to be safe within the school's walls. Bianca Elaine Lebron, born on June 26, 1991, to Carmelita Torres and Roberto Lebron, was a vivacious and loved member of her family in Bridgeport, Connecticut. Living with her mother and stepfather, Angelo Garcia, Bianca was part of a warm and caring family unit, including a younger sister Janiessa, with whom she shared a deep bond, a brother, and an older sister.

Described as outgoing and confident, Bianca easily made friends, loved to chat and laugh, and wasn't shy about meeting new people. Her hobbies were as vibrant as her personality; she adored dancing and singing, often seizing any opportunity to indulge in these passions. She also had a penchant for shopping, frequently visiting local malls, and had a beloved pet hamster named Nina. Purple, the color of royalty and creativity, was her favorite.

In the academic realm, Bianca shone brightly. Her school records painted the picture of a diligent, well-behaved student with a keen intellect. She seldom missed school, and her teachers regarded her as an enthusiastic and capable learner. Her mother, Carmelita, fondly recalled how Bianca prioritized her homework, always ensuring it was completed before she indulged in playtime. Neighbors, like Amy Colon, remembered Bianca as a beautiful, ever-happy child, often seen riding her bike or playing tag, a burst of joy in their community.

Yet, on that fateful morning, as Bianca left with the mysterious man in the van, a chilling reality set in. Her family, unaware of her absence from school, expected her to follow her usual routine: attending classes, then visiting a relative or a friend's house. The police later suggested that the confusion surrounding her disappearance might have stemmed from her flexible after-school schedule, which varied day-to-day.

It wasn't until around 4:30 p.m., a full eight hours after Bianca was last seen by her classmates, that her family realized something was amiss. At first, there was no immediate alarm; but as time passed, concern grew into a harrowing realization that Bianca, their beloved daughter and sister, had vanished.

Several months prior to her mysterious disappearance, Bianca Lebron had once been the subject of a minor scare. In January, she had briefly gone missing, only to be found hours later at a friend's house, simply having lost track of time. This incident, seemingly innocent and resolved quickly, perhaps contributed to the initial lack of urgency when Bianca didn't return home on that November day. It wasn't until the day's light began to fade into the evening that concern started to mount among her family.

Carmelita, Bianca's mother, began a frantic search to locate her daughter. She made numerous calls to friends and relatives, but none had seen Bianca that day. It was around 8:30 pm, a full twelve hours since Bianca was last seen, when her sister revealed a crucial piece of information. She hadn't seen Bianca at school that day, which was unusual because they normally crossed paths. This revelation propelled Carmelita into further action, intensifying her search efforts. After exhausting all other options, she finally made the call to the Bridgeport Police to report her daughter missing, around 10:24 pm.

It's crucial to note that Bianca's family was completely unaware of her absence from school that day. They had not been informed of the story Bianca had told about an uncle taking her shopping. When the police arrived at the family's Clinton Avenue home, Carmelita recounted the morning's events, the last time she saw her daughter, waiting with her older sister and four cousins to walk to school. Later, in a heart-wrenching statement to the media, Carmelita expressed her torment and confusion, unable to fathom why this tragedy befell her daughter and family, a pain that she lived with every day.

The police, upon taking the missing person's report, noted several critical points. First, it was highly uncharacteristic of Bianca to skip school, especially without her family being notified. Their investigation at Elias Howe School revealed a startling truth and a series of failures in the school's policy and procedures, which would later become the focus of a civil suit filed by Bianca's family.

According to the school's policies, Bianca's teacher was required to verify her absence when Bianca mentioned her uncle picking her up. This procedure was mandated whenever a child was to be taken from school grounds by someone other than a legal guardian. However, this crucial step was overlooked. Sonia Salcido, the school superintendent, expressed deep regret and horror over this lapse in protocol, acknowledging the gravity of the situation. The teacher was subsequently suspended, pending an investigation into why these protocols were not followed.

The police now faced a daunting task. Bianca had been missing for over 12 hours, and they had little to work with. Interviews with Bianca's friends yielded the story about her uncle, but upon questioning her family, it became evident that Bianca might have used the term "uncle" more loosely, possibly referring to a family friend or an older acquaintance rather than a legal relative.

Despite the scant details about the man who picked up Bianca, witnesses provided a comprehensive description. He was a Hispanic male, aged between 20 and 30, standing between 5 feet 8 inches and 5 feet 11 inches tall, with a medium build. His distinctive features included black curly hair styled in a semi-afro, long sideburns, a beard, brown eyes, a prominent nose, and noticeable scratches on his cheeks. He wore a long-sleeve blue pullover shirt with the "GAP" brand, FUBU brand jeans with a Fat Albert cartoon character on the right rear pocket, and scuffed brown Timberland boots. Notably, he made no attempt to conceal his identity while picking up Bianca.

The van used in the abduction was equally distinct: a two-tone brown or possibly beige, in poor condition with sanded areas, body damage, tinted windows, and chrome trim. With these descriptions, police were able to produce a composite sketch of the man, which they distributed widely in hopes of finding leads.

The police, after speaking with witnesses and school administration members, returned to Bianca's family with unsettling news. They learned from the family that Bianca had no uncle matching the description of the man who picked her up, nor did they know anyone who owned a van resembling the one described. This information steered the police towards treating the case as a likely non-familial abduction, focusing their efforts on locating both the mysterious van and its driver, believed to be Bianca's abductor.

The rarity of such an abduction, particularly from a school at the beginning of the day, was not lost on the investigators. Such incidents are usually linked to custody disputes, but in Bianca's case, there was no such dispute. Both her parents, Carmelita and Roberto, were united in their efforts to find Bianca, tirelessly searching and plastering the town with flyers.

Sergeant Jesus Ortiz of the Bridgeport Police Department's Youth Bureau, who was at the forefront of the investigation, faced the daunting task of piecing together limited information. Despite the widespread distribution of flyers and substantial media coverage, the majority of the tips and leads that came in led to dead ends. Ortiz remarked on the challenging nature of the investigation, noting the team's diligence in pursuing every lead, no matter how small or uncertain.

As the weeks turned into months with few developments, the police continued to actively work the case, though without significant breakthroughs. In December, a month after Bianca's disappearance, a potential sighting in Pittsburgh, Pennsylvania, sparked a glimmer of hope. However, this lead fizzled out as the sighting could not be confirmed as Bianca, and no further sightings were reported.

For Bianca's family, particularly her mother Carmelita, the ordeal was a living nightmare. Carmelita's days and nights were consumed with efforts to find her daughter, from distributing flyers to confronting the school board. She blamed the school for Bianca's abduction, arguing that it happened under their watch due to their negligence. In a desperate move to pursue legal action against the city, Carmelita faced the agonizing decision to have Bianca legally declared dead, a step she took in April 2002, just five months after the abduction. This decision was seen as unusual and hastened by many, including Sergeant Ortiz, who found it strange but not suspicious.

Around the same time, the investigation took a disturbing turn when 20-year-old Jason Lara emerged as a person of interest. Lara, disturbingly referred to as Bianca's "secret boyfriend" in some reports, was a troubling figure due to the vast age difference. Allegations surfaced that Bianca had a crush on Lara, and there were reports of inappropriate interactions between them. The connection was even more concerning because Bianca's great-uncle was in a relationship with Lara's mother, providing a link between the two.

Further deepening the suspicion was the fact that Lara had a friend who owned a van matching the description of the one seen during Bianca's abduction. Bianca's grandmother, Sonia, acknowledged that Bianca knew Lara but downplayed the nature of their relationship, considering Bianca's young age.

Despite having a potential suspect, the police faced a significant obstacle: Lara had left Bridgeport shortly after Bianca's disappearance and his whereabouts were unknown. Complicating matters, Lara had previously been fingerprinted under a different name, constituting forgery. His criminal history, which included an attempted carjacking conviction, added to the urgency of finding him. In an effort to track him down, a warrant was issued for his arrest for second-degree forgery, following a news article that brought renewed attention to his potential involvement in the case.

In April of 2003, a significant turn occurred in the investigation of Bianca Lebron's disappearance when Jason Lara, the man previously identified as a person of interest, initiated contact with the Bridgeport Police. In a phone call laden with mystery, Lara spoke to the authorities but refrained from revealing his location. He firmly denied any involvement in Bianca's disappearance, although the police were able to trace his call to Fort Myers, Florida. This discovery led to a collaboration between the local Florida authorities and the Bridgeport Police, culminating in Lara's apprehension in November, two years after Bianca vanished. Unable to post the substantial bail set at $100,000, Lara was extradited back to Connecticut for questioning.

This development was a significant breakthrough for the investigators. They had not only multiple witnesses describing a close, albeit deeply inappropriate relationship between Lara and Bianca, but he also bore a strong resemblance to the artist's composite sketch of the suspect. Sheila Santiago, speaking on behalf of the Bridgeport Police Department, conveyed the importance of Lara's arrest, suggesting he possessed crucial information pertinent to the case. However, Lara proved to be a challenging individual to extract information from, cooperative yet elusive in his responses.

During this time, Lara was residing with his fiancée, Corey Vedi, and their young son in Florida. Vedi staunchly defended Lara, dismissing the allegations linking him romantically to Bianca as baseless. She claimed that Lara had not seen Bianca since the summer before her abduction, a timeline that positioned him away from Bianca for months prior to her disappearance.

Despite the accumulation of circumstantial evidence and suspicions, the authorities faced a roadblock: they lacked sufficient evidence to formally charge Lara with any crime related to Bianca's disappearance. After extensive questioning, Lara provided an alibi for the time of Bianca's abduction, which, upon verification, appeared solid and unbreakable. The specifics of this alibi remained undisclosed, leaving many to speculate about the veracity of Lara's statements.

Lara's brush with the law did not end there. In 2011, he faced arrest on unrelated burglary charges. This incident prompted the police to approach him again regarding Bianca's case, but Lara remained reticent, declining to comment further. The police, without legal grounds to compel his cooperation, were left at an impasse.

Six and a half years after Bianca's disappearance, a settlement was reached between her family and the city of Bridgeport in response to the wrongful death suit filed by the family. The city agreed to a settlement of $750,000, to be paid to the family in six annual installments of $125,000. This settlement, while acknowledging the city's mishandling of the situation, brought little solace to the family. Angelo Marcos, the attorney representing Bianca's family, emphasized that no amount of money could compensate for the ongoing anguish and the unresolved nature of Bianca's case.

In August 2009, a new lead emerged when state police, acting on information received during an unrelated case, conducted a search in Seaside Park, located near Bianca's school. The tip suggested that the remains of a young girl might be buried there, raising the possibility that it could be Bianca. However, after an extensive search, no human remains were found, and the lead ultimately led nowhere.

Detective John Burke, who later took over the case, inherited a daunting amount of information: over 50 boxes filled with reports, tips, and leads. Despite the overwhelming odds, Burke remained dedicated to finding answers, acknowledging the slim chance of finding Bianca alive but refusing to give up hope.

Over the years, various tips and leads have surfaced, including one that took investigators as far as New Mexico, but each has been a case of mistaken identity or a dead end. Outside of the suspicions surrounding Jason Lara, no other suspects or persons of interest have been named in the case.

Bianca Elaine Lebron has been missing since November 7, 2001. At the time of her disappearance, she was a 10-year-old Hispanic female with brown hair and hazel eyes, standing 4 feet 11 inches tall and weighing approximately 115 pounds. She was last seen wearing a green, beige, and camouflage shirt, beige pants, black boots, and a dark blue denim jacket, and was picked up in a distinct two-tone brown van outside her school in Bridgeport, Connecticut.

Her father, now living in Florida, regularly returns to Bridgeport to search for his daughter and uses social media to share her story. Carmelita, Bianca's mother, remains haunted by the absence of her daughter, holding onto hope despite the overwhelming odds. The memories of Bianca, still vivid and painful, drive her family's continued search for answers, refusing to give up in the face of an enduring mystery.

Jaylen Griffin

In the vibrant city of Buffalo, New York, nestled within the Broadway-Fillmore area, a young boy named Jaylen Griffin came into the world on April 22nd, 2008. Born to his loving mother, Joanna, Jaylen was the youngest member of the family, a position that often came with extra love and attention. His arrival marked a joyful addition to a close-knit family unit, where he was embraced with open arms and hearts filled with affection.

Growing up, Jaylen was known as a 'mama's boy,' a term that fondly reflected his deep bond with his mother. His family, including a doting grandmother who resided next door, formed a supportive and nurturing network around him. This circle of care and guidance played a significant role in shaping Jaylen's childhood, making it one filled with happiness, freedom, and a sense of security.

The city of Buffalo, expansive and bustling, was both Jaylen's home and playground. Despite its size, the community in which Jaylen lived was tight-knit, a characteristic that was especially evident in his neighborhood. Here, Jaylen spent his early years, reveling in the simple joys of childhood and growing into a kind-hearted and well-loved young boy.

The summer of 2020 brought with it the challenges of the ongoing pandemic, altering life in ways both big and small. Despite these changes, Jaylen, who had just completed fifth grade, found ways to stay engaged and active. One of his favorite activities was visiting the local grocery store on his street. Here, he would offer to help customers with their bags, a small service for which he was often rewarded with a bit of spare change or a small payment. This task was more than a way to earn pocket money for Jaylen; it was an opportunity to connect with his community and lend a helping hand, showcasing his burgeoning sense of responsibility and kindness, even at the tender age of 12.

August 4th, 2020, dawned like any other summer day for Jaylen. The family had recently welcomed a new puppy, adding more joy and excitement to their home. That morning, Jaylen eagerly took the puppy out for a walk, a routine that filled him with delight. After returning home, he informed his mom of his plans to head back outside, casually asking if she needed anything from the store. The store, a familiar and frequented spot, was just a short walk from their house. His mother, accustomed to Jaylen's frequent trips there, thought nothing of it, assuming he was off to earn some extra money as he often did.

However, as the day turned into night, and the darkness enveloped the city, Jaylen had not returned. The store had closed, and there was no sign of him anywhere. His family, gripped by worry and fear, acted quickly, calling the police to report him missing and seeking assistance in finding their beloved boy. Unfortunately, the initial response from the authorities was not as urgent as the family had hoped. Mistakenly believing Jaylen to be a runaway, the police did not immediately launch a full-scale search.

The response of the authorities to Jaylen's disappearance was, at first, disappointingly lackluster. They seemed convinced that Jaylen, a young boy of only 12, had simply run away from home. Their advice to his distraught parents was to wait, suggesting that he would likely return on his own in a day or two. This approach, however, did not sit well with Jaylen's family. They knew him better than anyone – a cheerful, content child reveling in the joys of summer, proud of his newfound ability to earn a little money, and deeply bonded with his family and his new puppy. Running away was out of character for Jaylen, and his family was certain of it.

Jaylen's mother, Joanna, firmly believed that her son would never voluntarily leave. With the police not fully invested in the search, the responsibility fell heavily on the family, friends, and the local community. They embarked on a determined and extensive search operation. Moving from door to door, they spread the word about Jaylen's disappearance, posting flyers wherever they could. However, this endeavor was not only emotionally draining but also financially taxing for a family already struggling with resources.

Despite these challenges, the search for Jaylen continued tirelessly. Every now and then, a glimmer of hope would appear in the form of a tip or a reported sighting. The family and volunteers would spring into action, flooding the reported neighborhood with inquiries and additional flyers, yet these efforts often led to dead ends. The uncertainty of where to search next was daunting. Jaylen was last seen at his home in the Broadway-Fillmore neighborhood and possibly at the nearby grocery store, but beyond that, his whereabouts remained a mystery.

As days turned into weeks, the family's heartache deepened, and concerns grew that Jaylen might have been lured or taken against his will. While the police response remained minimal, two organizations stepped forward to offer substantial support: The Community Action Coalition of Western New York (CACWNY) and the "Bury the Violence" initiative.

CACWNY, a beacon of hope for those facing adversity, extended its resources and expertise to Jaylen's family. They provided missing person posters, flyers, and helped organize structured searches. Their confidential tip line became an essential tool, receiving and promptly acting upon any leads regarding Jaylen's sightings.

"Bury the Violence," founded by Karima Morris following a personal tragedy, became another pillar of support. The organization, dedicated to finding missing children and combating community violence, played a pivotal role in raising awareness about Jaylen's case. They organized searches, coordinated with volunteers, and amplified the call for assistance in finding Jaylen.

Buffalo, New York, a city steeped in history and culture, is a significant urban center on the western edge of the state. It stands proudly on the banks of Lake Erie, its grandeur second only to New York City in terms of urban population in the state. With over 275,000 residents, Buffalo is a bustling hub, a stone's throw away from the natural wonder of Niagara Falls and the Canadian border, adding to its geographical allure.

Despite its impressive size and proximity to international borders, Buffalo faces its share of challenges. The city, known for its high crime rates, scores a mere 7 out of 100 on NeighborhoodScout's safety index, placing it in a precarious position in terms of public safety. This is a city where every shadow and every street corner tells a story, not all of them pleasant.

Amidst these urban challenges, human trafficking statistics have become a grim focal point. Although reports suggest an increase in trafficking incidents, authorities believe this spike is not necessarily indicative of more crimes but rather an increase in reporting. This shift is largely attributed to the efforts of organizations like Bury the Violence and the Community Action Coalition, which have been instrumental in raising awareness and aiding in the reporting of such crimes.

Buffalo is not just a city defined by its struggles. It has reinvented itself in recent years, emerging as a cultural hub. Renowned museums, universities, and tourist attractions dot the landscape, showcasing a vibrant, more hopeful side of the city.

As for connectivity, Buffalo offers an array of travel options. With a major airport, train depots, bus stations, and access to several major highways, the city is a nexus of transportation. Located near Lake Erie and Canada, it offers unique geographical advantages as well.

Within this diverse and complex cityscape lies the Broadway-Fillmore neighborhood, a community on the lower east side where Jaylen Griffin lived. His street, Warren Avenue, is a typical residential area, characterized by its walkability and proximity to major thoroughfares.

On August 4th, 2020, Jaylen's life took an unexpected turn. He left his home, intending to visit a nearby store, but whether he ever reached his destination remains a mystery. The subsequent months brought more tragedy to the Griffin family, with Jaylen's older brother Jaan tragically losing his life. Despite these hardships, the family held onto the hope that Jaylen, who was exceptionally close to his family, would return, especially after hearing of his brother's passing. But he never did.

This period was a time of introspection and change for Buffalo, especially regarding how missing children cases were handled. The initial approach of waiting 24 to 48 hours before commencing a search was critically reevaluated, recognizing that every moment is crucial in such situations. The city's police force, acknowledging the need for immediate action in cases of missing children, has since adopted a more proactive stance.

In this context, the disappearance of Jaylen Griffin raises several poignant questions. Did he make it to the store he mentioned? Are there any CCTV footages or confirmed sightings of him? What insights could his electronic devices or friends provide about his intentions that day? Despite numerous tips and sightings reported, the mystery of what happened to Jaylen Griffin on that fateful summer day remains unsolved, leaving a void in the hearts of his family and community and a series of unanswered questions that continue to echo through the streets of Buffalo.

Jaliek Rainwalker

J aliek Rainwalker's life journey began in Albany, New York, on August 2nd, 1995. Albany, as the state capital, lies on the picturesque west bank of the Hudson River, about 135 miles north of the bustling streets of New York City. With a vibrant community of nearly 100,000 residents, Albany presents a rich tapestry of history and culture.

The circumstances of Jaliek's birth are shrouded in mystery and heartache. Information about his early life is scarce, with many details either undisclosed to the public or lost in the mists of time. What is known, however, paints a picture of a challenging start to life. Jaliek was born into a world where his mother was battling addiction to crack cocaine, a reality faced by an alarming number of children during the devastating crack epidemic of the 1980s.

The impact of prenatal cocaine exposure on children has been a subject of intense study and debate. In Jaliek's era, there was a widespread belief that such exposure led to severe developmental issues, including significantly reduced mental capacities and major social problems. As scientific understanding has evolved, it's become clear that these children often face behavioral challenges, cognitive deficits, particularly in speech and memory, and altered brain function in areas related to attention and language. The full extent of these impacts continues to be explored through ongoing research.

Jaliek's life took a dramatic turn just two days after his birth on his mother's kitchen floor, when he was placed for adoption. His early years were marked by the struggle to overcome the effects of his prenatal cocaine exposure. This manifested in violent temper tantrums, during which he became inconsolable, often alarming other children and foster parents alike. By the age of seven, Jaliek had already been through six foster homes, a testament to the challenges posed by his early life experiences and the revolving door of the foster care system.

Jaliek's journey through the foster care system was under the umbrella of therapeutic foster care, a specialized system designed for children with significant social, behavioral, or emotional needs. This system pairs children with foster parents who have received specific training to handle such complex cases, providing a more nurturing and effective environment than traditional foster care or residential treatment facilities.

Despite the specialized care, Jaliek's journey was fraught with difficulties. He displayed symptoms indicative of an attachment disorder, a condition marked by an inability to form strong emotional bonds with caregivers. Children with this disorder often exhibit a range of challenging behaviors, including withdrawal, sadness, lack of interest in social interactions, and an inability to seek or respond to comfort. Managing a child with both attachment disorder and a propensity for violent outbursts is a daunting task, even for the most experienced and dedicated foster parents.

The Shoen family, Jaliek's sixth foster family, were committed and caring foster parents who even began the adoption process. For four years, they provided Jaliek, nicknamed "J," with a stable and loving home. Jaliek showed signs of a bright and curious mind, particularly in his love for reading and fascination with dinosaurs. However, the challenges of managing his violent outbursts became increasingly overwhelming for the Shoens, especially after a particularly alarming incident involving one of their daughters. With heavy hearts, they made the difficult decision to end the adoption process and return Jaliek to the state for re-placement.

In 2002, Jaliek entered what would be his final foster home, with Steven Kerr and Jocelyn McDonald in Greenwich, New York. This small, predominantly Caucasian town in upstate New York presented a new backdrop for Jaliek, who was of African-American and Caucasian descent. Kerr and McDonald, who had already adopted a daughter and had three biological sons, welcomed Jaliek with open arms, hopeful to integrate him into their family.

In the quaint town of Greenwich, New York, Jaliek "J" Rainwalker seemed to have found a semblance of stability and happiness in the home of his adoptive parents, Steven Kerr and Jocelyn MacDonald. After a tumultuous early life, marked by constant transitions between various foster homes, J's adoption by Kerr and MacDonald appeared to be a beacon of hope, a promise of a permanent and nurturing family environment.

However, beneath the surface of this seemingly idyllic setting, concerns were brewing. J's adoptive grandparents, Dennis Smith and Barbara Reilly (MacDonald's mother), harbored apprehensions about the family dynamics. Initially, they believed that Kerr and MacDonald had the best intentions for J. However, as time passed, they began to question whether those intentions remained steadfast, especially during periods when J's behavior became challenging.

The adoption process itself is rigorous, involving meticulous scrutiny of the prospective parents, home inspections, and numerous visits. The child, in this case J, also undergoes psychological counseling to ensure a smooth transition into the new family. However, once the adoption is finalized, the intense oversight gradually diminishes, leaving the well-being of the child primarily in the hands of the adoptive family. Smith and Reilly expressed concerns that, over time, Kerr and MacDonald's commitment to J may have waned, especially during difficult periods.

Allegations and hearsay swirled around the treatment of J and his adopted sister compared to Kerr and MacDonald's biological children. It was rumored that while the biological children enjoyed more freedom, toys, and late nights, J and his sister faced more restrictive conditions, such as early bedtimes and limited access to toys. Kerr and MacDonald refuted these claims, insisting they treated all their children equally and did their utmost to support J.

Their living conditions also raised eyebrows. The family's choice of a "non-traditional lifestyle" involved living in a 20x20 foot cabin with no running water, outhouses instead of restrooms, and limited electricity from a generator. This lifestyle, aimed at being environmentally friendly, presented a unique and unconventional setting for raising a family.

J's journey with his adoptive family grew increasingly complex. By 2007, at the age of 12, he was described in the media as being thin and gangly, standing 5 feet 6 inches tall but weighing only 105 pounds. Kerr and MacDonald reported growing difficulties in managing his behavior, which included severe outbursts and concerning psychological issues. Despite these challenges, there were no reports of J being returned to counseling or receiving any medical treatment to help manage these problems.

In a critical turn of events, on October 23rd, 2007, Steven Kerr made a frantic call to a crisis hotline. He expressed his struggles with managing J's behavior, which had reportedly escalated to include threats of violence and sexual aggression. Kerr even inquired about the possibility of reversing the adoption, a testament to the gravity of the situation.

The counselor on the hotline suggested respite care as an alternative to reversing the adoption. Respite care provides a temporary break for both the family and the child, offering a chance to recalibrate and address issues in a less charged environment. J was no stranger to respite care, having previously spent time with Elaine and Thomas Person, a couple experienced in fostering children with complex needs.

The Persons, who had fostered over 45 children, were well-versed in handling attachment disorders and other behavioral challenges. They described J as a sweet and intelligent child, despite his behavioral problems. After a brief stay with them, plans were made to transfer J to another respite home. However, before this could happen, J returned to the care of his adoptive parents and spent a night with Kerr in his parents' home on Hill Street in Greenwich.

The decision to bring J to this particular location, away from the rest of the family, remains a subject of speculation. Some believe it was to avoid further disruption before his next stint in respite care, while others wonder if it signified a deeper rift within the family dynamic.

Some conjectured that Jocelyn MacDonald, J's adoptive mother, had reached her limit in coping with J's challenges and was therefore opposed to his return to their home. This theory added a layer of complexity to the already bewildering circumstances surrounding J's vanishing.

Further complicating the narrative, conflicting reports emerged about the home where J was last seen. Owned by Steven Kerr's parents, some accounts suggested the elder Kerrs lived there and discovered J's disappearance upon finding his bed empty. Other reports indicated the Kerrs did not reside there at the time, leaving only J and his father present. Yet another version posited that the Kerrs were out of town. Amidst these varying accounts, one fact remained constant: Steven Kerr was the last person known to have seen J alive on the evening of October 31st, 2007.

Kerr reported that he put J to bed that night, and everything seemed normal. However, the following morning, on November 1st—the day J was scheduled to go to another respite home—Kerr found his son's bed empty. J had apparently left a note expressing remorse and a desire to no longer be a burden. This discovery set off a frantic search by Kerr, who called out for J and scoured the neighborhood before reporting his son missing to the police at 8:57 a.m.

Initially, it was presumed that J, grappling with personal troubles and the prospect of returning to respite care, had run away. The police promptly initiated an extensive search operation, broadcasting J's description across local media. The story rapidly gained national attention, drawing offers of assistance from various organizations and individuals, including many of J's former foster parents, who were deeply concerned about his well-being.

Kerr's home, nestled in a remote area with dense woods and lakes, presented a challenging environment for a search. The harsh winter conditions of upstate New York compounded the urgency of finding the twelve-year-old. Despite the concerted efforts of police, state troopers, and volunteers using helicopters, tracking dogs, ATVs, and infrared cameras, no trace of J was found.

Adding to the mystery, Kerr later revised his account of finding J's bed empty, stating that J had actually attempted to conceal his absence by stuffing clothing and pillows under the blankets. This detail, alongside the note J left, painted a confusing picture of his intentions.

As the investigation progressed, the police grew increasingly suspicious of the circumstances surrounding J's disappearance. Both Kerr and MacDonald were questioned extensively. While MacDonald cooperated with a polygraph test, which she passed, Kerr refused to undergo the same. This refusal, coupled with inconsistencies in his statements, raised eyebrows among the investigators.

For instance, Kerr's account of his movements on the night of J's disappearance conflicted with phone records and eyewitness testimony. Surveillance footage from a bank in Glens Falls, captured hours before J was reported missing, showed a van resembling Kerr's passing by, contradicting his claim of staying at home all night. Despite these discrepancies, authorities were unable to definitively link the van to Kerr.

In the months following J's disappearance, the Rainwalker family made the unexpected decision to move to West Rupert, Vermont, a stark contrast to the behavior typically observed in families of missing children, who often maintain a semblance of stability in hopes of their return. When questioned about their cooperation with the investigation and their move, Kerr offered evasive responses, expressing frustration with the authorities and their handling of the case.

As the investigation unfolded, authorities grappled with inconsistent accounts and elusive leads. Steven Kerr, J's adoptive father, was perceived by law enforcement as evasive and possibly deceptive in his statements. In contrast, MacDonald, J's adoptive mother, was viewed as more straightforward in her interactions with the authorities.

A critical twist emerged when the Persons, the family who provided respite care for J just before his disappearance, challenged the theory that the note found by Kerr indicated J had run away. They suggested that the note, which Kerr presented as evidence of J's intention to leave, was actually written while J was in their care as part of an apology for his behavior, not as a farewell message.

The relationship between authorities and Kerr and MacDonald became increasingly strained. MacDonald's parents, Dennis Smith and Barbara Reilly, reportedly lost communication with their daughter and son-in-law after siding with the police, who suspected Kerr might hold key information about J's fate.

Throughout the subsequent months, various tips and sightings led to extensive searches but yielded no concrete results. One significant lead prompted the use of cadaver dogs at the Baton Kill Country Club, where the dogs reacted to a small pond. Despite draining the pond, no remains were found. Searches also extended into Vermont, exploring areas the family was known to frequent.

In a bizarre turn, an anonymous note received by a newspaper suggested J was alive and had been picked up along Route 40. The cryptic and disjointed message led to speculation and further investigation but ultimately did not provide a clear direction for the case.

By February 2008, Kerr was named a person of interest. As time passed, the possibility of finding J alive diminished, and the investigation's focus shifted. On the fifth anniversary of J's disappearance in 2012, Investigator Gloria Coppola announced a significant change: the case was now being treated as a presumed homicide.

In a poignant revelation, J's yellow fleece pullover, previously described as part of his last known attire, was recovered by his adoptive grandmother in the family's old home and handed over to the authorities. Despite exhaustive searches, including the Hudson River and properties in Troy (where Kerr's phone had pinged), no substantial evidence was found.

Amidst these efforts, J's family moved away from the area, settling in West Rupert, Vermont. This decision, along with their lawyer's guarded statements, added to the aura of mystery surrounding the case.

Years passed with the case gradually fading from the public eye, yet a dedicated group, including J's adoptive grandparents and former foster parents, continued to seek answers. They formed a task force, offered a substantial reward, and kept J's memory alive through billboards and flyers.

In 2016, a glimmer of hope emerged when a hiker discovered a skull along the Hudson River. Initially thought to potentially belong to J, it was later determined to be unrelated, dashing the hopes of investigators and those yearning for closure.

Prosecutors and law enforcement officials have expressed their commitment to the case, acknowledging the existence of evidence but also their cautious approach to avoid jeopardizing a potential future trial. The case remains a poignant reminder of the challenges in solving complex missing persons cases.

Two main theories have persisted: one that J left of his own accord but met with foul play, and the other that Kerr knows more than he has revealed. Despite the suspicions and scrutiny, Kerr has consistently denied involvement in his son's disappearance. J, described as a biracial boy with a unique appearance and speech impediment, remains a figure of enduring mystery and concern.

His case stands as a poignant symbol of resilience in the face of adversity and the enduring hope for answers in the midst of uncertainty. The story of Jaliek Rainwalker is a mosaic of challenges, care, and unresolved mysteries, continuing to haunt those who seek the truth behind his disappearance.

Erin Marie Gilbert

Erin's story begins in the vibrant city of San Francisco, California, where she was born on the 4th of May 1971. Her life, full of potential and promise, was tragically cut short, and today, she would have been on the cusp of her 49th birthday. Standing tall at 5'11 and weighing around 145 pounds, Erin was a striking figure with her Caucasian heritage, lustrous brown hair, and captivating hazel eyes.

Her beauty was not just skin deep; Erin's inner radiance shone through in every aspect of her life. As described in the gripping Alaska Unsolved podcast by Stephanie, Erin was a paragon of talent and intelligence. Excelling both in academics and sports, she was a force to be reckoned with. Her prowess on the basketball court was matched only by her skill in volleyball, painting the picture of an athlete who was as versatile as she was dedicated.

But Erin's talents were balanced with a profound sense of kindness and responsibility. She carried these traits with a confident air, setting an example for those around her. Growing up as one of three sisters, Erin shared an unbreakable bond with her siblings. The trio, known for their close-knit relationship, navigated their childhood in Everett, Washington with their mother, forging memories that would last a lifetime.

The winds of change brought Erin back to her birth city of San Francisco to live with her father, while Stephanie, her sister, embarked on a new life in Anchorage, Alaska with her husband and son. They settled at the Elmendorf

Air Force Base, a place that would soon become a significant part of Erin's story.

In the autumn of 1994, Erin found herself at a crossroads, uncertain about the path she wanted to take in life. Sensing her sister's indecision, Stephanie extended an invitation to Erin to come to Alaska, offering her a chance to explore new horizons. Erin embraced this opportunity with open arms, moving to Alaska and taking up a job as a nanny for a family known to Stephanie. Her future seemed bright, with plans to attend beauty school looming on the horizon.

Erin's life in Alaska was initially centered around Stephanie, her husband, and their circle of friends. However, as time passed, she yearned to forge her own path and meet new people. This desire led her to the famous Chilkoot Charlie's bar in Anchorage, a decision that would alter the course of her life. It was here that she met Dave Combs, a man who would play a pivotal role in the unfolding events.

Their connection sparked quickly, and soon Dave invited Erin to the Girdwood Forest Fair on the 1st of July, 1995. The fair, a beloved annual event in Girdwood, Alaska, was known for its eclectic mix of Alaskan artists, handcrafted items, exotic foods, and entertainers. It was a celebration that drew crowds from all over, breathing life into the resort town known primarily for its winter skiing.

Girdwood, a safe haven where residents could stroll at night without fear, was about to be the backdrop of an unimaginable incident involving Erin. On the fateful day, Dave picked Erin up from Stephanie's house on the Elmendorf Air Force Base around 4 PM.

On that fateful day, Erin and her date, Dave, set out from the Air Force Base, embarking on a journey that would lead them to the bustling Girdwood Forest Fair. The fair, nestled at mile 2.2 on the scenic Alyeska Highway, was about a 55-minute drive according to modern Google Maps. Erin, with an eye for style, was dressed perfectly for an outdoor adventure – her attire included a chic black leather jacket, a black and white striped shirt, rugged mountain boots, and classic black jeans.

Their arrival at the fair was marked by a blend of excitement and curiosity. Around 5:30 p.m., Erin was spotted engaging with a vendor at a hair design and face painting table. Her interest was piqued by the idea of getting a bellybutton piercing, a fashionable statement of the times. Although the vendor wasn't offering piercings that day, they noted down Erin's details, showing her keen interest in the idea. This interaction, detailed in the riveting Alaska Unsolved podcast, provides a glimpse into Erin's vibrant personality.

The podcast also sheds light on the man accompanying Erin – described by the vendors as having a clean-cut, military-style appearance, which seemed at odds with Erin's more relaxed style. This contrast sparked curiosity among the vendors, leading one to speculate on the podcast whether the man with Erin was indeed Dave, who was known to have long hair when he picked her up.

The investigation into Erin's disappearance delved into this discrepancy. The police explored this angle, but it didn't lead to any conclusive evidence. The prevailing belief was that the man at the vendor table with Erin was indeed Dave.

Later, around 6:15 p.m., the couple was seen in the beer garden by six of Dave's friends. After some time, these friends departed for a dinner party at a nearby cabin, leaving Dave and Erin to head back to his car around 6:45 p.m. It was at this point that the evening took an unexpected turn.

According to Dave, they discovered that his car battery was dead, a result of accidentally leaving the lights on. He suggested to Erin that he would walk to a friend's cabin nearby to seek help. Dave's journey, which he claimed lasted two hours, was fruitless – he couldn't locate the cabin. When he returned to the car, Erin was nowhere to be found. Strangely, upon his return, the car started without issue.

Dave's subsequent actions add to the mystery. He claimed to have returned to the fair, searching for Erin until about 1:00 a.m., but she was nowhere to be found.

In 1995, Dave shared with the Daily News his thoughts on the night Erin disappeared. He had assumed she might be upset with him and left on her own. The following morning, with a sense of unease, Dave reached out to Stephanie at 7:00 a.m., inquiring if Erin had returned home. To his dismay, Stephanie confirmed Erin was not there. The untouched state of Erin's room was a clear indication that she had not come home that night. Stephanie, deeply concerned, felt something was amiss. It was uncharacteristic of Erin not to inform her if she needed help or a ride.

Determined to find Erin, Stephanie and her husband took immediate action. They drove down to the Girdwood Forest Fair the very next day, hoping to find any trace of her. In a desperate attempt to locate Erin, they even had her name announced on stage, urging attendees to keep an eye out for her. They combed through the festival and the neighboring woods, but their search was fruitless. Their call for assistance from the state troopers was met with an unsettling silence; no help arrived for several days.

Three days into Erin's disappearance, Stephanie and her husband, feeling helpless, turned to the media. It was only then that the police began to actively engage in the search. On July 6th, a comprehensive search operation was launched. State troopers, aided by search dogs and helicopters, scoured the area. They meticulously inspected the woods, considering the possibility that Erin, being a newcomer to Alaska, might have ventured out on a hike. However, knowing Erin's sensible and responsible nature, it seemed unlikely she would wander into the woods alone.

Erin's last known whereabouts were amidst a bustling crowd, making her sudden vanishing all the more perplexing. Standing at 5 feet 11 inches, with a slim build, Erin was someone who would stand out in a crowd. Her athletic background suggested she would not go down without a fight. The mystery deepened: how could someone of her stature and strength disappear without a trace in such a populated area?

A 2018 article on Medium.com highlighted a chilling statistic: since 1988, over 60,700 people had been reported missing in Alaska. This equates to an alarming average of five people per 1,000 residents reported missing each year, with an average of 2.25 people disappearing every year – a rate twice the national average in the USA. Erin's case was just one among thousands.

The high number of missing persons in Alaska can be attributed to various factors. The state's vast and wild terrain attracts adventurers from around the world, eager to explore its natural beauty. It also serves as a haven for those seeking to escape the law or personal obligations. Alaska is a land of extremes: extreme weather, rugged nature, and formidable predators. The ease with which one can get lost in such an environment is a grim reality, often leading to tragic outcomes.

Lieutenant Randy McFerrin, the dedicated investigator on Erin's case, high-lighted the challenges of conducting searches in Alaska. The vast and rural terrain of the state can make it difficult to locate missing persons, a reality that often doesn't involve foul play. In many cases, the harshness of nature is to blame. However, for Erin, the circumstances suggested something more ominous.

In the days following her disappearance, searches were conducted, but no trace of Erin was found. Speculations about her possibly taking an impromptu trip were quickly dismissed; it was uncharacteristic of Erin to leave without notice. The fact that she never reappeared lent credence to the belief that her disappearance was not voluntary.

The last person known to have been with Erin was Dave Combs. However, it is crucial to note that he has never been officially considered a suspect in the case. Despite this, his actions and statements have raised questions. Lieutenant McFerrin indicated that multiple attempts to contact Dave for further questioning have been unsuccessful. He provided initial statements but has since remained out of touch with both the authorities and Erin's family.

The lack of concrete evidence against Dave or any other suspect leaves the case shrouded in mystery. Questions about the thoroughness of the investigation into Dave, including whether his car was searched or scrutinized in detail, remain. Dave's visit to the police station for a polygraph test, which he left before completing, adds another layer of intrigue.

With limited evidence and no body, it's challenging to determine if Erin's disappearance was an accident or a result of foul play. The case hinges on the discovery of new evidence or a breakthrough lead, such as the unfortunate discovery of human remains.

Erin's case is one of many handled by Alaska's Cold Case Investigation Unit. Established in 2002 with federal grants, the unit initially consisted of four detectives tasked with solving over a hundred cases dating back to the 1950s. Despite early successes, funding issues led to its discontinuation in 2015, only to be reopened in 2017 with Lieutenant McFerrin as the sole detective. His efforts, hindered by limited resources, focus on reanalyzing evidence with modern technology.

The case raises numerous unanswered questions. For instance, why did Dave leave Erin alone for two hours? Was he seen during this time? And is it possible for a car battery to spontaneously start working after being flat for hours? These questions, along with many others, are explored on the Finding Erin Marie Gilbert Facebook page, where Stephanie has listed 20 questions she wishes to ask Dave.

Despite the lack of solid leads, Erin's family remains determined to uncover the truth. They have offered a $35,000 reward for information leading to the arrest and conviction of those responsible for Erin's disappearance. The Alaska State Troopers continue to seek any information, no matter how small, encouraging the public to come forward.

The case remains open, a testament to the enduring hope for answers and justice in the mysterious disappearance of Erin Gilbert.

LaTonya Roberts

LaTonya Roberts' journey through life was as vibrant and dynamic as the lush, green landscapes of Broward County, Florida, where she was born on a sunny Tuesday, October 10, 1972. Her arrival marked a joyous moment for her parents, Virgil and Ernestine, blessing them with their second daughter. The family's tapestry was woven with the laughter and love of several girls, with LaTonya nestled in the heart of this close-knit circle, where the age gap between siblings never exceeded six years.

Growing up, LaTonya's spirit was a blend of sweetness and playfulness, a sparkle that shone bright in the Florida sun. She was a child of diverse interests, equally happy when cradling her dolls in a world of make-believe, as she was when racing her bike down the winding paths, her fingers trailing through the earthy richness of the soil. Her home was a sanctuary of joy and creativity, echoing with the sounds of laughter and the busy patter of little feet.

Music flowed through the Roberts household like a melodic river. Virgil, a devout Pentecostal preacher, instilled in his daughters a deep love for singing. The church choir was where LaTonya and her sisters found their voices, their harmonies soaring through the rafters, touching the hearts of all who heard. Their father's role as a minister, combined with his job as a custodian at Palm Lake Elementary School, anchored the family in a community rich with faith and humility.

In 1984, the family's journey took them northward, over 200 miles from the sun-kissed shores of Fort Lauderdale to the vibrant heart of Central Florida's Orange County. They settled in a cozy home along CA Grande Drive, nestled close to the serene expanse of Cypress Grove Park. Here, in Orlando, LaTonya blossomed from a playful child into a thoughtful, charismatic teenager, her days filled with the familiar rhythms of high school life at Oak Ridge High.

LaTonya's teenage years were a kaleidoscope of experiences and emotions. Her warm, inviting personality drew people to her, and she navigated the halls of high school with a circle of friends always by her side. As she matured, her beauty and charm caught the attention of many, but LaTonya remained focused, undistracted by the flurry of adolescent romance. Her heart was set on her dreams and aspirations, her eyes fixed firmly on the horizon of her future.

After graduating from Oak Ridge in 1990, LaTonya wasted no time in pursuing higher education. She enrolled at Orlando College, diving into the realms of business and medicine with her usual fervor and dedication. Her academic journey was marked by high grades and a clear vision for her future. Soon after, LaTonya embarked on her professional path, joining the PCA Family Medical Center as a medical assistant. This role not only fulfilled her career aspirations but also kept her close to her beloved family home.

In the fall of 1994, after two and a half years of commendable service at the Medical Center, LaTonya's face graced the local newspapers, featured in articles discussing medical policies and health insurance issues in Florida. Tragically, this rise in public visibility would soon be overshadowed by a harrowing turn of events.

It was in December of that same year that the vibrant light of LaTonya's life would be shrouded in mystery. Conflicting reports circled around the date of her last sighting - some saying December 14th, others the 16th. For clarity's sake, December 16th, a day marked by the typical warmth and humidity of Central Florida, is acknowledged as the last day LaTonya was seen.

That day, she was excited for an evening event - her sister Lolita was to sing the National Anthem at a basketball game at Oak Ridge High School. LaTonya, ever the supportive sister, arrived with a video camera, ready to capture Lolita's moment of glory. However, after receiving a page from her boyfriend, LaTonya left the game early to meet him. This would be the last time Lolita would see her sister.

Later that night, around 11:00 p.m., Lolita received a call from LaTonya, who invited her to join her at a local club. But the conversation was strained; tension was apparent from LaTonya's boyfriend in the background. This phone call, fraught with underlying tension, and a subsequent discussion about a movie outing with another sister, would be the last interactions LaTonya would have with her family.

In the days that followed, a cloud of uncertainty and fear descended upon the Roberts family. LaTonya's disappearance became the focal point of a desperate search, her absence leaving a palpable void in the hearts of her loved ones. The once joy-filled home on CA Grande Drive was now shrouded in anxious silence, as the family grappled with the inexplicable vanishing of their beloved daughter and sister.

The evening she vanished, LaTonya had been equipped with a video camera to capture her sister's singing performance at a basketball game. This camera, later found back at her family's residence, served as a silent testament to her return home after the game, but before her journey to her boyfriend's house. This finding, coupled with her conversation with Lolita about visiting her boyfriend, and his voice heard in the background of the 11:00 p.m. call, led everyone to believe that she did indeed make it to her boyfriend's place that night. However, the events that unfolded after 11:00 p.m. remain shrouded in enigma, forming the crux of a mystery that has persisted for nearly three decades.

LaTonya's absence from home was not immediately alarming. As a young adult, she was afforded the liberty to come and go as she pleased. However, when Saturday rolled around with no word from her, the seed of worry began to sprout among her sisters. Attempts to reach out to her friends and family yielded no clues to her whereabouts, escalating their concern. Adding to the tension was the fact that their parents, Virgil and Ernestine, were away on a church mission trip and were not due back until Sunday.

By Sunday, a sense of foreboding had firmly taken hold. LaTonya, known for her dedication to her job and unlikely to miss work without notice, had now been unaccounted for two full days. This was not only uncharacteristic but deeply alarming. Upon their return, Virgil and Ernestine were quickly enveloped in the growing panic. Their attempts to reach out to LaTonya's boyfriend only heightened the hysteria when he claimed he hadn't seen her since Friday night.

In a desperate bid to find their beloved daughter, the family divided their search efforts. They targeted the movie theater she might have planned to visit and Club Heroes, where she had mentioned going. Virgil's search led him to the vibrant melon red facade of Club Heroes, located at 426 East Kennedy Boulevard in Eatonville. The club, under new management and now known as Club Koha, was quiet in the early hours of Sunday, offering no clues. Virgil then extended his search along Kennedy Boulevard, where fate led him to a chilling discovery – LaTonya's car, a white four-door 1988 Toyota Corolla, parked near the corner of East Kennedy and Yore Road.

The car, locked and with its security system armed, presented a puzzling scene. There were no obvious signs of a struggle or forced entry, though one tire was mysteriously flat. The lack of foreign objects in the tire left investigators baffled as to whether it was a routine puncture or a deliberate act to immobilize the vehicle. The circumstances under which the car was found were undeniably suspicious.

The investigation quickly escalated from a mere missing person case to something more sinister. A deep dive into LaTonya's life revealed a young woman flourishing in her personal and professional spheres. She was well-liked, had a close circle of friends, a loving family, a rewarding job, and a healthy savings account. There were no signs of her planning to leave or any indication of turmoil that would lead to her disappearance. The police were left grappling with a perplexing case: a missing woman with virtually no evidence or leads to explain her sudden vanishing.

Witnesses were scarce, and none reported any unusual activity or distress. Employees and patrons at Club Heroes could not recall seeing LaTonya on the night in question, casting further doubt on whether she ever made it there. The absence of any sightings or reports left a haunting void, a narrative incomplete, with more questions than answers.

As investigators delved deeper into the mysterious disappearance of LaTonya Roberts in December 1994, they were confronted with a perplexing detail that cast doubt on the assumption that she had been the one driving her car on that fateful night. LaTonya, a petite woman standing just under 5 feet, had unique driving habits due to her stature. To comfortably reach the pedals and have a clear view of the road, she would pull the driver's seat forward to its maximum and sit atop a thick blue cushion for added height. However, when her car was found, the driver's seat was pushed all the way back, and the cushion that was always in the driver's seat was now on the passenger seat. This anomaly raised a critical question: had someone else been driving LaTonya's car that night?

The peculiar positioning of the driver's seat and the misplaced cushion suggested a taller person's involvement, leading detectives to ponder over the possibility that LaTonya might not have been alone or even in control of her vehicle when it was abandoned. The haunting uncertainty of whether she was a passenger in her own car that night, and if so, why the last person to see her hadn't come forward, deepened the mystery.

Detectives were candid in their communication with the media, stating that while there was no concrete evidence of foul play, the circumstances surrounding LaTonya's disappearance left few other plausible explanations. Known for her strong family ties and work ethic, the idea of LaTonya vanishing without a trace and not contacting her family was both out of character and alarming. The lack of leads and evidence left investigators with little to work on. Initial inquiries suggested no clear enemies or individuals who might wish to harm her, pointing towards the possibility that her disappearance involved either a stranger or someone from the outskirts of her social circle.

However, the case took a dark turn when LaTonya's sisters disclosed unsettling details about the months leading up to her disappearance. They painted a picture of a life marred by stress, trauma, and pain, predominantly stemming from her tumultuous relationship with her boyfriend. Described as rocky at best, it was revealed that the relationship was rife with both physical and emotional abuse. LaTonya, meticulous in documenting her life, had kept extensive notes in her diary and planner about the assaults and the psychological trauma she endured at the hands of her boyfriend. These writings also revealed her efforts to seek help, including regular visits to a therapist.

A particularly harrowing incident about a month before she went missing brought a new dimension to the investigation. As recounted by her sisters, LaTonya had been abruptly awakened by her boyfriend one night and taken on a chilling drive to a remote citrus grove in Haines City, some 40 miles from Orlando. There, under the cloak of darkness, he forced her out of the car at gunpoint, leading her deep into the grove. He menacingly gestured towards a human-sized hole he had dug, threatening her life and making it explicitly clear that any future transgressions would result in her disappearance, with no chance of her being found.

This disturbing revelation compelled investigators to reclassify LaTonya's case from a simple missing person to a missing endangered individual. They now faced the grim possibility that her boyfriend might have acted on his previous threat. The question loomed large: could he have been responsible for her disappearance, possibly hiding her body in an obscure location like the citrus grove? Alternatively, was it conceivable that despite living in constant fear within an abusive relationship, LaTonya had fallen victim to a random act of violence by someone else she encountered that night, maybe at the club or from a more distant part of her social network?

Nearly three decades after the disappearance of LaTonya Roberts, the complexity and mystery surrounding the case continue to puzzle investigators and haunt her family. The question of what happened to LaTonya on that fateful night in December 1994 remains unanswered, despite the passage of time and the evolution of investigative techniques.

One of the most perplexing aspects of the case revolves around the investigation into LaTonya's boyfriend. Despite his being a significant figure in her life and having previously threatened her, astonishingly little is known about him publicly. Even his name remains undisclosed. Detectives, in their attempts to glean information from him, were met with a wall of silence, as he denied knowledge of LaTonya's whereabouts and refused to cooperate further. This lack of cooperation, coupled with the disturbing details of their relationship, particularly the incident in the citrus grove, casts a shadow of suspicion over him. Yet, without concrete evidence or more information, investigators found themselves at a standstill.

The Orange County Homicide Detectives, Leonard and Nazerchuk, undertook the daunting task of searching citrus groves in the vicinity of Haines City in Polk County. The area, known for its sprawling citrus groves, presented them with a monumental challenge akin to finding a needle in a haystack. They combed through the groves on foot and surveyed the area from helicopters, looking for any signs of disturbed earth or hidden graves. Despite their extensive efforts, they came up empty-handed, their hopes of finding a clue or trace of LaTonya dashed.

As months turned into years, the case grew cold. The leads that had once seemed promising dwindled, and the investigation hit a dead end. The boyfriend remained an avenue for further investigation, but the lack of developments over the years and the decision to keep his identity private diminished the hopes of a breakthrough.

In June of 2020, the case saw a glimmer of hope as new investigators were assigned to re-examine it. Sergeant Ben Thorp, who managed the domestic violence and missing persons unit for the Orange County Sheriff's Office, and Sergeant Gloria Morris, known for her work on cold missing persons cases, brought fresh eyes to the investigation. Despite their expertise and determination, significant progress remained elusive, and the case continued to be a heart-wrenching mystery.

The family's pain and longing for answers have been unrelenting. The thought of LaTonya being alive and possibly in captivity, or worse, dead and buried in an unknown location, is a source of constant anguish. They hold onto the hope that one day they will have the answers they so desperately seek and the opportunity to bring LaTonya home, to grieve and memorialize her properly.

LaTonya's sister, Lolita, reflects on the enduring impact of her disappearance, expressing the deep emotional toll it has taken on her and her family. The sense of loss and the unresolved nature of the case continue to be a daily burden, a haunting presence in their lives.

For nearly 30 years, the mystery of what happened to LaTonya Diane Roberts remains unsolved. At the time of her disappearance, she was a young black female with brown eyes and brown hair styled in braids, standing 4 feet 11 inches tall and weighing approximately 90 pounds. She was last seen wearing a black leather jacket, a fuchsia-colored flower print shirt, purple stretch pants, black boots, and possibly an Oak Ridge High School class ring from 1989 or 1990. She may have also been carrying a brown Dooney and Bourke purse. Her white four-door 1988 Toyota Corolla was later found near the intersection of

East Kennedy Boulevard and Yore Road.

As the years pass, the mystery of LaTonya's fate continues to echo through the hearts and minds of those who knew and loved her. The enduring hope for closure, for justice, and for the truth about what happened to LaTonya Diane Roberts remains a fervent wish for her family and friends.

Terrance Williams

errance Dion Williams, a man with a past colored by both adversity and resilience, entered the world on January 17, 1976, in the bustling city of Chattanooga, Tennessee. Born to Marsha Williams and a father who vanished from his life when he was merely three, Terrance's early years were marked by a noticeable absence. Despite this, he carved a path through life, albeit one that wasn't always smooth.

In 1995, a young Terrance faced the harsh realities of the judicial system. He found himself entangled in legal troubles, pleading guilty to a robbery charge. This resulted in an 11-month sentence, partially served as probation, and an additional 50 days in jail following a DUI charge and driving with a revoked license. These experiences, though challenging, were pivotal chapters in Terrance's life story.

Seeking a fresh start and the comfort of family, Terrance moved to the sunny landscapes of Florida, drawn closer to his mother Marsha. Their bond was a strong one, manifesting in daily phone calls and cherished moments spent together. They often embarked on leisurely drives to local malls, where they would meander through stores and enjoy dinners, relishing each other's company. Terrance, sharing an apartment with a roommate at Randall Circle in East Naples, found solace in this new chapter of his life.

Professionally, Terrance turned a new leaf, starting work as a cook at a Pizza Hut restaurant in Bonita Springs, Florida. This was a departure from his previous construction jobs back in Tennessee. But life had more twists in store for him.

On the night of January 11, 2004, Terrance, a man known among his Pizza Hut co-workers for his warmth and friendly demeanor, attended a party at a house in Bonita Springs. The night was filled with camaraderie, beer, and laughter, lasting until the early hours of the morning. Terrance, undeterred by his lack of a valid driver's license and an expired car registration, had driven to the party illegally, a decision born out of necessity rather than recklessness.

When Terrance failed to return home, concern quickly set in. Jason Gonzalez, his roommate, alarmed by his absence, reached out to Marsha on January 13th. The worry was palpable, leading the Williams family to file a missing person's report with the police.

In a twist of fate, Terrance's aunt discovered his Cadillac, which had been towed from Naples Memorial Cemetery for obstructing traffic. The tow report bore the signature of Deputy Steve Caulkins from the Collier County Sheriff's Department. This discovery set off a chain of events that plunged the Williams family into a deepening mystery.

Further inquiries revealed an unsettling scenario. Cemetery workers recalled witnessing Deputy Caulkins pull over Williams, conduct a pat-down, and then place him in the back of the patrol car before driving away. The Cadillac was later returned to the cemetery, with the car keys mysteriously found on the ground beside it.

The Williams family, desperate for answers, repeatedly contacted the Sheriff's Department, seeking information from Deputy Caulkins. Initially, Caulkins claimed no memory of any arrests or towed cars on the day of Williams' disappearance. However, when pressed further, his story changed, and he claimed a clearer recollection of his encounter with Terrance.

The supervisors of Deputy Steve Caulkins, a central figure in this enigmatic case, requested that he provide a detailed incident report to shed light on his interactions with Williams. Caulkins' report, penned with an air of officialdom, offered a narrative that only deepened the mystery.

According to Caulkins, his encounter with Williams began at approximately 12:15 PM. He claimed to have noticed Williams' car exhibiting signs of distress, a situation that prompted him to follow the vehicle. The pursuit led them to a cemetery parking lot, where a peculiar exchange supposedly took place. Caulkins reported that Williams, appearing hurried and anxious about being late for work, requested a ride to a nearby Circle K convenience store. This detail, however, struck a discordant note, as it was later confirmed that Williams had no employment ties with the Circle K.

After allegedly dropping Williams off at the store, Caulkins returned to the Cadillac left in the cemetery. He claimed to have searched the vehicle's glove compartment for paperwork, only to find that the proper registration was missing. Feeling deceived, Caulkins said he used his work-issued cell phone to call the Circle K, seeking to speak with Williams. The store clerk, however, supposedly informed him that Williams was not an employee there. This revelation led Caulkins to check the car's license plates, which he found to be expired.

However, as the investigation unfolded, the veracity of Caulkins' account came under intense scrutiny. Forensic analysis of phone and surveillance records painted a vastly different picture. Notably, there was no evidence of Williams or Caulkins appearing on the surveillance footage from the Circle K. This discrepancy raised serious doubts about Caulkins' claims of dropping Williams off at the store.

Further undermining Caulkins' narrative were the findings from his cell phone records. Contrary to his report, there was no recorded call made to the Circle K. This inconsistency cast a shadow over his version of events, suggesting that vital elements of his story were fabricated.

Moreover, the employees of Circle K were thoroughly interviewed, but none could corroborate Caulkins' story. No witnesses could place either Caulkins or Williams at the store during the time frame in question. This lack of corroboration from independent sources added another layer of complexity to the case.

Felipe Santos, a 24-year-old Mexican national, found himself in a precarious situation, living illegally in the United States. By the time of his mysterious disappearance, he had been in the U.S. for three years, working diligently in Florida. His days were spent laboring with a singular goal in mind: to send money back to his family in Mexico, a noble endeavor that showcased his dedication and familial love.

Santos' life took an unexpected and dramatic turn on October 1, 2003. It was a typical morning, around 6:30 AM, and he was on his way to work, accompanied by his two brothers. Their routine was abruptly disrupted when they became involved in a minor car accident in Naples. The incident caught the attention of Deputy Steve Caulkins, who, upon arriving at the scene, cited Santos for reckless driving and for lacking both a driver's license and insurance. In a move that would later become a focal point of controversy, Caulkins placed Santos in the back of his patrol car. This was the last time Felipe Santos was seen.

Later that day, a bewildering discovery was made. Santos' employer, concerned for his employee, contacted the county jail to post bail, only to find that Santos had never been booked. Caulkins offered a perplexing explanation for this. He claimed that he had a change of heart about the arrest because Santos was polite and cooperative. According to Caulkins, he left Santos at a local Circle K and simply drove off.

However, this account was directly contradicted by the other driver involved in the accident. She reported that Caulkins seemed agitated by Santos' lack of documentation, expressing frustration about repeatedly encountering drivers without licenses. Her statement painted a different picture of the events, casting doubt on Caulkins' version.

Two weeks after Caulkins submitted his incident report, Santos' family, deeply concerned and without any news, filed a missing person's report. They also filed a complaint against Caulkins. Despite these efforts, an investigation into the matter cleared Caulkins of any wrongdoing. Since that fateful day, Felipe Santos has vanished without a trace.

The handling of Santos' disappearance raised serious questions, particularly from his wife. She highlighted the seemingly cursory nature of the investigation, pointing out that she had never been interviewed by the investigators. This omission added to the growing suspicion surrounding the case.

Further doubts were cast on Caulkins' credibility when a recording of his call to dispatch, regarding the towing of William's car, came to light. In the recording, Caulkins described the car as abandoned and obstructing traffic. This description starkly contradicted both his incident report and witness statements, which indicated that Caulkins himself had moved the vehicle to the location where it was blocking the road.

Caulkins' behavior during the call further muddied the waters. He was heard joking, "Maybe he's out there in the cemetery, he'll come back, and his car will be gone." He also used inappropriate language, referring to the car as a "homie Cadillac." When questioned about these discrepancies and his choice of words, Caulkins defended his actions, claiming he was just joking around with a friend and insisting that his moving the car was merely an attempt to assist the towing company, rather than an effort to make the vehicle appear abandoned.

In a twist that further complicated the already intricate case of Terrance Dion

Williams' disappearance, Deputy Steve Caulkins made a perplexing move about 20 minutes after his initial encounter with Williams. He requested a background check on Williams, but with a crucial error - he provided an inaccurate birth date. This was no ordinary mistake; the date he gave was one that Williams had used during a previous arrest. This revelation starkly contradicted Caulkins' earlier claims that he never knew Williams' last name or any other personal details, casting further doubt on his credibility and intentions.

Given the gravity of the situation and the involvement of a police officer as the main person of interest, the case escalated beyond local jurisdiction. The Florida Department of Law Enforcement and the FBI were brought in, a decision that underscored the seriousness of the investigation. Their involvement brought new investigative techniques to the forefront. Notably, a covert operation was launched, which included the placement of a GPS device on Caulkins' vehicle, a move straight out of a detective thriller. Additionally, a thorough forensic investigation of the patrol car was conducted, leaving no stone unturned in the quest for clues.

In an effort to unearth more evidence, cadaver dogs were employed. These specially trained dogs scoured areas identified by the GPS data, but, disappointingly, their searches yielded no further evidence, deepening the mystery.

The case took a significant turn when Caulkins was fired from the department. His dismissal was due to providing conflicting information about the disappearances of both Williams and Santos, and his lack of cooperation with the investigation. This development added another layer of intrigue to the already complex case.

For years, the case languished without any significant breakthroughs, until a resurgence of interest in 2012. National media programs, including Anderson Cooper 360 and Dateline NBC, began covering the story, bringing renewed attention to the unsolved mysteries. This media spotlight amplified public interest and scrutiny.

In a remarkable display of advocacy and support, entertainment mogul Tyler Perry took a vested interest in the case. He appeared on Al Sharpton's MSNBC talk show to discuss the disappearances, bringing his considerable influence to bear. Perry's involvement was not just in words; he offered a substantial reward of $100,000 for information connected to the cases. This generous act by Perry underscored the ongoing quest for justice and answers in the mysterious disappearances, rallying public support and keeping the stories of Williams and Santos in the national conversation.

Ann Riffin

Ann Riffin's life unfolded like a tapestry of contrasts and introspection, beginning on a serene Sunday, May 8, 1949, in New Jersey. Born to Irving, a respected physician, and Babette, an intellectually precocious woman who finished high school at 15, Ann was the second melody in their familial symphony, arriving three years after her sister Jane. The Riffins, a Jewish family, resided in the affluent suburbs of Montclair, New Jersey, a town known for its picturesque charm and proximity to the bustling life of Essex County.

Babette, affectionately known as Babs, was a pillar of the community, dedicating her time and intellect to various local causes, including the Board of Education and the Public Library. Meanwhile, Irving's medical career earned him considerable respect. The Riffins instilled in their daughters a deep devotion to their faith, with Babs also actively participating in the board of their local temple.

Ann, in her early years, was often described as a contemplative and thoughtful child, contrasting sharply with her sister Jane, who was more academically driven and involved in extracurricular activities. Ann harbored a soulful creativity, often seen drawing, painting, writing, and collecting wildflowers. Her affinity for the natural world was profound; she sought to encapsulate its beauty and majesty through her art and writings, expressing her deep connection to the world around her.

Her parents, in later interviews, often drew comparisons between Ann and her sister. One particular article in the Albuquerque Journal highlighted these differences, noting Jane's competitive and assertive nature in contrast to Ann's more introspective and expressive demeanor. Babs reminisced about how Jane, at 12, was a magnet for young suitors, while Ann seemed disinterested in such adolescent social rites.

Ann's high school years at Montclair High School marked a shift; she began to mirror her sister's engagement in extracurricular activities. Her senior yearbook was a testament to her involvement, listing her as the student faculty attendance secretary, information officer of the Mountie Movement, Junior Council Mountaineer, editor-in-chief of the National Honor Society, and an associate editor for both the Mountie Handbook and Whirlwind, among other roles.

Following her 1967 graduation, Ann continued her journey at Wellesley College, a prestigious private women's school in Massachusetts. Yet again, her path paralleled and diverged from Jane's. While Jane achieved the honor of Phi Beta Kappa, Ann, though performing admirably, faced an internal struggle with her identity and career direction.

As Ann grappled with her future, Jane's life seemed to follow a more conventional path of marriage, career, and motherhood. This difference possibly fueled a competitive undercurrent, the origins of which—personal ambition or familial pressure—remained ambiguous. Irving, when questioned about possible jealousy between the sisters, suggested it wasn't overt, hinting at a complex dynamic.

Ann's decision to leave Wellesley during her junior year wasn't driven by family dynamics or academic challenges but by the tumultuous era of the Vietnam War. College campuses were erupting with activism and protests, and Ann, a soul too gentle for such strife, found herself torn by the chaos of both the war overseas and the unrest at home. Babette poignantly reflected on this, noting Ann's struggle to understand the violent times she lived in.

Retreating to Marblehead, a quaint town on Massachusetts' North Shore, Ann redirected her energies towards writing. She penned a book centered on the themes of peace and global unity, a testament to her longing for a harmonious world. In a bold move, Ann sent her manuscript to Apple Records, the label founded by The Beatles. To her astonishment, the label expressed interest and invited her to England to finalize her manuscript. While Ann embraced this opportunity and journeyed to England, her book, a reflection of her peaceful aspirations, unfortunately, never reached publication.

Despite her shy and introspective nature, Ann harbored a deep-seated love for travel, an eagerness to explore the world's vast tapestry. By a relatively young age, she had already seen the historic lands of Europe and Japan with her family, and during her college years, she even ventured to the ancient landscapes of Peru. Yet, her father Irving observed that these worldly experiences didn't seem to alter Ann's inherent approach to life or broaden her perspective in the way one might expect.

Upon her return from England, Ann sought refuge back in her childhood home in Montclair, where she grappled with the direction of her life's path. It was during this period of introspection that she found herself leading a youth hostel bicycling group on a journey from Pennsylvania to Virginia. The historical allure of Williamsburg, with its restored village and echoes of the past, captivated Ann's imagination. However, her enthusiasm for the site's historical significance wasn't shared by the younger members of the group, leading to a sense of frustration and disconnection.

This experience in Williamsburg sparked a newfound aspiration in Ann. She envisioned herself as a history teacher, eager to ignite a passion for the past in young minds. Following this newfound calling, Ann enrolled at the College of William and Mary, delving into the world of anthropology. She graduated in 1974, at 25, and soon found a position teaching at a local middle school.

However, her journey in education was short-lived; after just a year, she found herself navigating away from the classroom, struggling with student management.

Ann's next chapter led her to a private school operated by the New Testament Church, an evangelical sect. This environment introduced her to Christianity, which gradually began to resonate with her, much to the concern of her Jewish parents. Her growing involvement with Christian beliefs and practices, including attempts to share these views with her family, marked a significant shift in her life's trajectory.

Ann's career continued to be a mosaic of diverse roles. She worked as a bookkeeper for a real estate firm, then as a private nurse for a child suffering from a fatal illness. The child's passing deeply affected Ann, prompting her to return once more to Montclair. This period was marked by a series of attempts to find her footing—enrolling in secretarial school, brief stints in New York City, and returning home when things didn't work out. Her parents, Irving and Babs, expressed concerns about what they perceived as Ann's lack of direction.

In a bold move to redefine her identity, Ann journeyed to Israel, embracing her Jewish-Christian beliefs. She worked as an editor for a scientific journal, learned Hebrew, and wrote articles for a New Jersey-based Jewish publication. However, this chapter too was short-lived, and Ann found herself back in Montclair, her aspirations of journalism unfulfilled.

The familial home became a pressure cooker of emotions and expectations. Invited to live with her sister Jane, Ann hoped this change of scenery would offer a fresh start. While she formed close bonds with her nieces and found solace in her artistic pursuits, tensions arose with Jane over Ann's seeming lack of ambition and drive.

As the 1980s dawned, Ann, in her 30s, found herself in a state of limbo, grappling with a deepening depression that began to eclipse her life. Her days were marred by an increasing reluctance to engage with the world. Babs recounted the growing concern as Ann struggled to find a reason to rise each morning.

In an effort to help, Ann's parents encouraged her to seek psychological counseling. As part of the therapeutic plan, they began charging her room and board, hoping to motivate her towards independence. Ann's plea to delay these charges until she secured a job was met with understanding yet firm encouragement from her parents to actively seek employment. However, this approach seemed to deepen her despair.

In the spring of 1982, Ann reached a pivotal moment. With a sense of resolution, she packed a few belongings into her white 1979 Chevy Chevette and departed from her family home.

Laden with the optimism of a new beginning, her parents, Irving and Babs, believed they knew her destination. Ann had given the impression of a brief trip to Pennsylvania to visit friends. Yet, the course of events took an unexpected turn when a postcard arrived from Oklahoma, followed by a surprising phone call from Ann herself, revealing she was in New Mexico and had accepted a job offer.

Ann's parents tried to embrace her decision with open arms, hoping this new venture would mark a turning point in her life. Ann's choice of New Mexico wasn't entirely out of the blue. Babs had once shared her own teenage experiences in the state, painting a picture of its enchanting beauty—a landscape that seemed fitting for Ann's nature-loving spirit and her fluency in Spanish.

Ann's arrival in Ruidoso, a quaint village nestled in Lincoln County adjacent to the Lincoln National Forest, seemed like stepping into a different world. The village, with its history steeped in the tales of Billy the Kid and the Lincoln County War, offered a backdrop of historical intrigue that might have appealed to Ann's love for history.

In Ruidoso, Ann found a job at Whispering Pines, a local restaurant known for its home-cooked meals and a favorite among tourists. Ruth Ellis, the owner, was puzzled by Ann's decision to work there, given her impressive background. Ann's role at the restaurant was humble yet diverse, involving everything from cleaning pots to setting tables. Ruth noted Ann's inquisitive nature about the business, yet her personal life remained a closely guarded secret.

A fortuitous arrangement saw Ann moving into a cabin with Joan Stokes, Ruth's sister and a fellow employee at the restaurant. Their living situation worked well, largely due to their opposite work schedules and limited interactions, which minimized potential conflicts. Ann's lifestyle was quiet and reserved; she spent her time painting, writing letters, and reading, eschewing the more social and outgoing activities typical of her peers.

Ruth observed that Ann's demeanor was atypical for someone in the restaurant business. Ann's conservative nature extended to her appearance and social interactions; she never dated, despite the presence of single men at her workplace. Ruth described Ann as sincere and kind but also somewhat naive, struggling to grasp humor and seemingly disconnected from the experiences her extensive travels should have imparted.

The details of Ann's life in Ruidoso remained shrouded in privacy. She shared little about her past or her daily activities, leaving her new friends, like her family, in the dark. Joan, her roommate, noted Ann's frugality, recalling only a single purchase of shoes during their time living together.

Credit card records later revealed that Ann made at least two trips to Albuquerque, but the purpose of these journeys remained a mystery. Ann's communications with her family, limited to weekly calls, offered few insights into her life in New Mexico.

As autumn approached, Ann mentioned to her mother a planned trip to Colorado Springs to visit relatives and celebrate Yom Kippur. This trip, set against the backdrop of her recent move and enigmatic lifestyle in Ruidoso, added another layer to the already complex tapestry of Ann's life.

She informed her roommate, Joan Stokes, and her boss at Whispering Pines, Ruth Ellis, about her plans for a vacation. Ann requested and received a two-week leave, and on Sunday, September 12th, she packed her belongings into her car and departed from the cabin she had shared with Joan for the last three months. This departure marked the beginning of a mysterious disappearance that would leave a trail of unanswered questions and speculation.

For the subsequent two weeks, Ann's whereabouts remained unknown. Her family, under the impression that she was on vacation, did not expect regular communication, and thus no immediate alarm was raised. It wasn't until the morning of Monday, September 27th, that the first clue in Ann's disappearance emerged. New Mexico State Police Officer Herman Silva was dispatched to investigate an abandoned vehicle in the Mora Valley area, a remote region known for its rugged terrain and sparse population.

The vehicle, a white 1979 Chevy Chevette with New Jersey license plates, was found parked off New Mexico Route 3, near the small community of Holman. The area, while scenic, was not a common destination for travelers or tourists. The placement of the car raised questions about Ann's intended route and purpose in the area. Theories ranged from a possible wrong turn leading her astray to a deliberate choice to explore the scenic landscape, perhaps to capture its beauty in her paintings.

Upon inspecting the vehicle, Officer Silva noted that it contained personal belongings, showed no signs of damage, and was locked—a situation that initially suggested car theft. However, when Silva contacted the Riffin family in New Jersey, it became clear that the car was not stolen but belonged to their daughter, Ann, who had been missing.

The discovery of the car transformed the situation from a simple case of an abandoned vehicle to a complex missing person investigation. The car was in good condition, with a quarter tank of gas remaining, and showed no signs of struggle or violence. Inside, investigators found clothes, uncashed checks, several of Ann's paintings, painting supplies, and a stack of letters from friends she had made in the New Testament Church. These letters, containing invitations for Ann to rejoin the church community, provided a new avenue for investigation.

The Riffins considered all possibilities, including that Ann might have been visiting a childhood friend, Linda Dutra, in Taos. However, Linda was unaware of any plans for Ann to visit and expressed concern about the route Ann may have taken. The Mora Valley, known for its peculiar history and perceived dangers, was not a recommended path for a lone traveler.

As the investigation progressed, detectives explored various leads, including inquiries into religious groups and cults in the area, but these efforts led to dead ends. Ann's sister, Jane, doubted the likelihood of Ann joining a cult, given her intelligent yet indecisive nature. The lack of conclusive evidence, compounded by weather conditions that had likely erased any physical traces, left investigators with more questions than answers.

The Riffins, unable to travel to New Mexico due to Irving's health issues, sent Lester Leave, a relative and lawyer, to assist with the investigation. Despite his efforts and those of the police, no significant progress was made in unraveling the mystery of Ann's disappearance. Witnesses provided vague and inconclusive accounts, and the peculiar circumstances surrounding the location where the car was found only deepened the mystery.

Lester Leave, determined to aid in the search for Ann Riffin, took proactive steps to reignite interest in her case. He commissioned flyers featuring photos of Ann and an appeal for information, offering a reward of five hundred dollars for any leads. The peculiar nature of Ann's disappearance, marked by a glaring absence of clues, made her case particularly memorable to the investigators involved. AP Wickard, one of the state police officers on the case, noted the unusual aspect of not receiving a single tip, despite the story being featured on news programs and Crime Stoppers.

The mystery of Ann's vanishing act seemed to deepen with time. Those in Ruidoso who had briefly crossed paths with Ann were taken aback by her sudden disappearance, yet they admitted to not knowing her well. She had always been reserved, rarely sharing details about her life. This lack of personal connection left a wide berth for speculation, with theories ranging from her possibly joining a religious group to becoming a victim of foul play.

Officer Silva, one of the first on the scene where Ann's car was found, was at a loss about what could have happened to her. AP Wickard expressed doubts about foul play but also acknowledged the bleakness of the situation, given the absence of any physical evidence. Time marched on, and the flyers with Ann's image became weathered and replaced, gradually fading into the background as new cases demanded the attention of investigators.

Two years after Ann's disappearance, in the summer of 1984, an unexpected figure from her past rekindled the search. R.D. Stewart, who knew Ann from her time in Williamsburg during the early 1970s, learned of her disappearance and was deeply troubled by it. Motivated by concern, he and his wife embarked on a journey through northern New Mexico, visiting small villages, distributing new flyers, and inquiring about Ann. One unverified sighting of a woman resembling Ann painting in the woods near Holman provided a glimmer of hope, but it led nowhere.

Stewart, grappling with the baffling nature of Ann's disappearance, considered all possibilities, including the haunting thought that she might have suffered from amnesia. In 1985, AP Wickard, still involved in the case, continued to pursue leads, however tenuous, including unidentified bodies and alleged sightings of Ann, but each lead ended in a dead end.

The Riffins, desperate for any clue, followed every possible lead, no matter how remote. One such lead emerged from an article in People magazine featuring England's Princess Anne visiting a clinic in Bangladesh. A nurse in a photo bore a resemblance to Ann, but this lead too was debunked when it was confirmed that the nurse was a local Bangladeshi woman.

The Riffins struggled with the ambiguity of Ann's fate. Babs grappled with feelings of guilt, wondering if her parenting style had impacted Ann's choices. The fear that Ann might have been harmed or that she was deliberately avoiding contact with her family weighed heavily on them. Irving, reflecting on Ann's mental state before her disappearance, couldn't dismiss the possibility that she might have chosen to harm herself.

The paintings found in Ann's car, now hanging in the Riffin's home, served as a poignant reminder of their daughter. Irving, analyzing these artworks, noted a shift in her style that he found troubling, drawing parallels with Van Gogh's later works.

Meanwhile, in New Mexico, locals like Dorothy Vigil, the Postmaster General in Holman, recalled the case with a sense of detachment. She noted the lack of local interest or information, a stark contrast to what might have been if Ann had been a local resident.

For those who knew and loved Ann, life moved forward, but her absence left an indelible void. The mystery of Ann Riffin, enveloped in a cloud of unanswered questions, remained a haunting enigma, a story of a life interrupted, leaving a trail of speculation and heartache in its wake.

Nathaniel Holmes

Nathaniel James Holmes entered the world on the crisp autumn day of November 5th, 2000, beginning his life's journey. He was the third of four children, nestled between two older sisters who doted on him and a younger brother who looked up to him. Nathaniel's early years were shaped by the strong family bonds he shared with his siblings and the adventures they embarked on together.

The Holmes household was a hub of activity and laughter, with the children's voices often echoing through the halls. However, the dynamics of this lively home shifted when Nathaniel was just eight years old. It was then that his parents, for reasons known only to them, decided to part ways. This pivotal moment marked a turning point in Nathaniel's life. Despite the divorce, the children remained primarily with their father, a pillar of strength and stability during this tumultuous time. Their mother remained a constant presence in their lives, with regular visits that kept the family ties strong.

The Holmes family, united in their love for adventure, journeyed far and wide. They traversed the diverse landscapes of Canada and Mexico, soaked in the historic charm of Scotland, and delved into the underwater wonders off the Virgin Islands. Perhaps the most memorable of their escapades was a month-long safari in the heart of Africa, an experience that left an indelible mark on young Nathaniel's heart and mind.

Amid these travels, Nathaniel discovered his passions. He was an avid video gamer, finding solace and excitement in the digital realms. His love for the outdoors was equally evident in his enthusiasm for hunting and fishing. Music, too, played a melodious part in his life, with Nathaniel showcasing a natural talent for it.

Yet, as Nathaniel navigated his teenage years, he encountered turbulent waters. School, a place where many find their footing, became a battleground for him. Shy and introverted by nature, Nathaniel often felt like a square peg trying to fit into a round hole within the school's walls. Recognizing his struggles, his parents made the decision in 2017 to shift him to homeschooling. However, this new educational path proved challenging for Nathaniel, who struggled with the self-discipline required for such an independent form of learning.

Around this time, at the age of 17, Nathaniel experienced a minor car accident, a fender bender that would have more significant repercussions. His father, Ben, concerned about Nathaniel's responsibility and focus, decided to restrict his access to the car. This decision came with a caveat – improve in school, and the car privileges would be reinstated. But improvement was elusive for Nathaniel, his struggles in education persisting.

In a twist of fate, a couple of Nathaniel's friends were attending an alternative school, Hidden Lake High School, located in the neighboring town of Westminster, Colorado. This school, known for its smaller class sizes, hands-on approach, and supportive environment, seemed like a beacon of hope for Nathaniel and his parents. After much deliberation, the decision was made to enroll him there, buoyed by the thought that he would be among familiar faces.

On the chilly winter afternoon of December 18, 2017, Nathaniel Holmes' life took an unexpected turn. His father, Ben, arrived at school to pick him up, immediately sensing that something was amiss. Nathaniel, usually vibrant and energetic, was uncharacteristically lethargic, his movements sluggish, his demeanor distant. Concern etched on his face, Ben prodded his son for answers, his parental instincts on high alert.

As they drove home, the silence in the car was palpable. Ben's mind raced with possibilities. Nathaniel's behavior was so out of character that Ben couldn't help but suspect that his son might have ingested something harmful. After relentless questioning, Nathaniel's defenses crumbled, and he confessed to taking Xanax, given to him by a friend at school. This revelation was a shock to Ben, who had never witnessed such behavior from Nathaniel. He believed his son's claim that this was his first foray into such substances.

Ben's worry deepened. That evening, he had work commitments he couldn't avoid, making it impossible to keep a watchful eye on Nathaniel. In a decision spurred by concern, Ben arranged for Nathaniel to spend the night at his mother's house, where she could monitor him closely. Before parting, Ben took away all of Nathaniel's money, hoping to cut off any potential access to more substances.

The following morning seemed to dawn with a return to normalcy. Nathaniel appeared to be in a decent mood, and it was his mother's turn to drive him to school. However, just as they were about to leave, Nathaniel realized he had forgotten an important folder at his dad's house. They made a quick detour, and Nathaniel dashed inside to retrieve it. Inside, he briefly encountered his sister, Hannah, who later recounted that Nathaniel seemed perfectly normal. He grabbed the blue folder and hurried back to the car, heading towards school.

However, Nathaniel's arrival at school was marred by tardiness, and his mother, concerned but hopeful, watched him enter the building before driving off. Inside, Nathaniel's behavior was far from ordinary. He loitered outside a classroom, anxiously trying to catch a friend's attention. The principal, noticing his unusual behavior, intervened, instructing Nathaniel to return to his class. Nathaniel protested, claiming an emergency, but the principal was firm. Nathaniel, rather than heading to class, made a choice that would escalate the situation: he left the school grounds and headed to a nearby park.

At the park, Nathaniel approached a stranger, requesting to use her phone. He left a voicemail for his mother, concocting a story about getting a ride with one of his dad's friends and spending time at their house. This message left his mother confused and concerned, prompting her to arrive at the school at the end of the day. But Nathaniel was nowhere to be found.

Alarmed, she contacted Ben, relaying Nathaniel's message about going to a family friend's house. Together, they unraveled Nathaniel's deception. A call to the school revealed that Nathaniel had never attended his classes that day. Ben, frustrated and concerned, questioned the school's policy on notifying parents of absences, learning that they opted for evening calls to ensure reaching a parent directly.

As the day waned, the mystery of Nathaniel's whereabouts deepened, his family's concern growing with each passing hour. The events of December 18 had taken a perplexing and worrying turn, leaving more questions than answers in their wake.

His parents, along with his siblings, tirelessly combed through every nook and cranny of their Colorado community, knocking on the doors of all of Nathaniel's friends. Each visit, however, only deepened the mystery, as no one seemed to have any inkling of Nathaniel's whereabouts. This was a bewildering situation for the Holmes family, as Nathaniel had never shown any tendency to run away or vanish without a trace.

Alarmed by Nathaniel's uncharacteristic disappearance, they promptly alerted the authorities. Unfortunately, the response from law enforcement was disheartening. Due to Nathaniel's age, they categorized him as a typical runaway, expected to return home soon. But Nathaniel's family felt a gnawing unease; they knew something was profoundly amiss.

In their relentless search for answers, the family learned about the troubling incident at school – Nathaniel's frantic attempt to communicate with a friend, claiming an emergency. This friend, when questioned, was baffled, having no idea what Nathaniel wanted or what the supposed emergency was.

Adding to the family's frustration was the school's lack of cooperation and transparency. The school failed to notify them of Nathaniel's absence on the day he disappeared, a fact that only amplified their anguish and worry. Nathaniel's friends, too, were at a loss, unable to provide any clues as to why he might have acted so peculiarly or where he could have gone.

The situation was exacerbated by the fact that Nathaniel had left without any personal belongings. He had no phone, no money, not even his ID. The only potential source of clues, his iPad, was found in his bedroom, but it was inaccessible. His father, Ben, tried repeatedly to unlock it, only to be thwarted and eventually locked out. The authorities, stretched thin and understaffed, couldn't offer much assistance in this regard.

Nathaniel's social media presence, which was minimal even before his disappearance, offered no clues, remaining completely stagnant. Driven by a relentless determination, the Holmes family continued their daily search. Ben, Nathaniel's father, took extraordinary measures in his quest. He discreetly drove through numerous homeless encampments across Colorado, using different vehicles to avoid drawing attention. He hung posters everywhere, spoke to everyone he encountered, and even played the bagpipes in public places – a tribute to Nathaniel, who was also a skilled bagpipe player, to raise awareness.

The search was punctuated by moments of fleeting hope. On one occasion, a young man resembling Nathaniel was spotted in Denver, carrying a tuba. Given Nathaniel's musical talents, this sighting seemed promising. However, upon investigation, no one matching Nathaniel's description was found. Another intriguing lead emerged from California, where a young man had borrowed a woman's phone and accessed the Facebook pages dedicated to finding Nathaniel and his father, Ben. Struck by the resemblance, the woman reported the incident, prompting Ben to rush to California within 18 hours, but again, to no avail.

With the Westminster police force overwhelmed and understaffed, Ben took the search into his own hands. He raised funds, enabling him to purchase surveillance equipment and drones to aid in the search. His ultimate goal was to gather enough resources to hire a private investigator.

Westminster, Colorado, nestled on the northern outskirts of Denver, is more than just a suburban city. It's a bustling hub with a vibrant population of over 100,000 residents, boasting a unique blend of urban and suburban lifestyles. This city, only a stone's throw away from the heart of Denver, sits merely 10 miles from the downtown area, making it an integral part of the larger metropolitan community. Adjacent to Westminster lies Arvada, Colorado, another suburban enclave where Nathaniel Holmes and his family called home. These two cities, Westminster and Arvada, though distinct, are seamlessly woven into the fabric of the Denver metropolitan area.

Nathaniel, residing in Arvada with his father and siblings, found himself traversing these interconnected communities daily. His educational journey led him to Hidden Lake High School in Westminster, an institution unlike traditional high schools. Known as an alternative high school, Hidden Lake offers a lifeline to students struggling to thrive in conventional educational settings, providing them a chance to succeed and graduate.

The school itself is situated in a lively part of Westminster, surrounded by a bustling four-lane highway, small businesses, and residential neighborhoods. This vibrant area is a hive of activity, a place where a 17-year-old walking alone might easily blend into the crowd, unnoticed by the busy passersby. The availability of public transportation options in Westminster – buses, trains – opens up a myriad of possibilities for travel, not only to downtown Denver but to far-reaching corners of the country. However, Nathaniel's disappearance was compounded by the fact that he had no ID on him, adding layers of complexity to the situation.

To the west of Denver lie the sprawling, majestic Rocky Mountains, a vast wilderness that stands in stark contrast to the urban landscape. Nathaniel's last known movements – leaving the school on foot, borrowing a phone at a nearby park – leave a trail that suddenly goes cold. The possibilities of what could have happened to him are numerous and troubling. Could he have gotten a ride from someone he knew, hopped on a bus, or even ventured on foot to an unknown destination? How could this young boy just vanish into thin air?

Many theories have circulated about Nathaniel's disappearance. Some speculate that he might have run away, overwhelmed by recent struggles. Despite his close ties with his family, the turmoil within a person's mind can often remain hidden. Authorities, considering his age and the lack of evidence pointing towards foul play, lean towards this theory. Yet, the possibility that Nathaniel might now be living among the homeless – a population he was known to interact with – cannot be discounted. With the transient nature of homelessness, he could be anywhere in the country by now, six years on.

Alternatively, there are darker theories. Could Nathaniel have met with an accident, perhaps related to substance use? Or might he have encountered foul play, hinted at by his frantic attempt to communicate with a friend and his nervousness when his mother confiscated additional Xanax pills? The school's apparent nonchalance about Nathaniel obtaining drugs, amidst rumors of a prevalent drug problem, adds another layer of concern.

Self-harm is another distressing possibility, but again, the question of his whereabouts remains unanswered. The prevailing theory among police and family is that Nathaniel chose to run away, possibly living among the homeless in Denver or beyond. Yet, for his family, this theory brings no solace. They struggle to understand why Nathaniel, part of a seemingly happy and close-knit family, would choose to disappear. His particularly strong bond with his older sister, just 11 months his senior, raises expectations that he might reach out to her, if only to assure her of his well-being.

The questions linger, hauntingly: Where could Nathaniel be now? What circumstances led to his sudden and mysterious disappearance? The answers remain elusive, shrouded in the complexities of a young life interrupted, leaving a family and community in a state of unresolved heartache and confusion.

Cherrie Mahan

The story of Cherrie Ann Mahan is a poignant tapestry woven with threads of love, resilience, and the unbreakable bonds of family, set against the humble backdrop of Saxonburg, Pennsylvania. Born on a warm summer's day, August 14, 1976, Cherrie entered a world that was as challenging as it was loving. Her mother, Janice Mahan, was a young girl of just 16 years when she embraced motherhood. Despite the daunting responsibilities that came with being a young mother, Janice's heart was filled with an immeasurable love for her daughter. She devoted herself completely to Cherrie, nurturing her into a child who was as friendly and talkative as she was beloved.

As Cherrie blossomed under her mother's care, their family circle expanded when Janice married LeRoy McKinney, a Vietnam veteran whose heart was large enough to envelop Cherrie as his cherished stepdaughter. In late 1984, in pursuit of new beginnings and the American dream, the family set down roots on Cornplanter Road in the picturesque Butler County. It was here, amidst the rolling hills and close-knit community, that Cherrie attended Winfield Elementary School. She was the kind of student who lit up the classroom with her bright smile and infectious enthusiasm. Her teachers and peers admired her for her intelligence, popularity, and the unbridled joy she brought into their lives.

The narrative takes a poignant turn on Friday, February 22, 1985. It was a day filled with the typical excitement and anticipation of an eight-year-old.

Cherrie was especially thrilled that day, buzzing with the joy of a promised playdate her mother had arranged for after school. The morning air was crisp as Janice and Cherrie made their way to the bus stop, a familiar and comforting routine for the pair. Located just fifty feet from the base of their home's uphill driveway, it was a short journey they had taken many times, each step a testament to their deep connection. As the school bus rolled up, Janice and Cherrie exchanged a tender moment, affirming their love for each other in a heartfelt farewell. Cherrie's bright eyes sparkled with happiness as she boarded the bus, waving goodbye to her mother, unaware of the uncertainty that lay ahead.

It all began on a cold winter afternoon, February 22, 1985, in the rural serenity of Cornplanter Road. Cherrie, a vivacious and beloved eight-year-old, stepped off her school bus at approximately 4:10 p.m., the world around her unaware that these moments would become a pivotal point in history.

Cherrie was not alone as she alighted from the bus; she was accompanied by three of her friends, their laughter and chatter filling the air with the carefree joy of childhood. Nearby, a car idled, driven by Debbie Burk, the mother of one of Cherrie's friends. Debbie had followed the school bus in her vehicle, a common practice in their close-knit community. As the other children climbed into Debbie's car, Cherrie embarked on her short journey home. She walked past a vehicle that seemed out of place in their tranquil neighborhood - a bluish-green van, parked ominously near the bus stop. This van, a 1970s-era Dodge, possibly a model from 1976, bore a distinctive mural: a skier boldly navigating a snowcapped mountain, a striking image against the van's muted colors. Unbeknownst to Cherrie, her every step was being observed from afar by Debbie Burk, the last person to see her before she vanished.

Cherrie, small in stature at just 4 feet 2 inches tall, with her brown hair and hazel eyes, was bundled up against the winter chill. She wore a gray coat, a blue denim skirt, a white leotard, blue leg warmers, and beige boots. Adding to her distinctive appearance were her Cabbage Patch earmuffs, a popular accessory of the time.

At the Mahan household, LeRoy McKinney, Cherrie's stepfather, had noticed the familiar sound of the school bus coming to a halt near their home. He contemplated walking down the 150-yard driveway to meet his stepdaughter, a gesture of care and routine. However, his wife, Janice, suggested otherwise, remarking, "No, it's a nice day. Let her walk." But as minutes ticked by and Cherrie did not appear, a sense of unease began to set in. Janice and LeRoy's worry escalated into fear as Cherrie remained missing. They initiated a search, hoping to find some trace of their daughter on the snow-covered path leading to their house. Their search, however, only deepened the mystery: Cherrie's footprints were nowhere to be found. The only clue was a set of tire impressions, etched into the driveway soil about fifty yards from their home, a silent testament to the unanswered questions surrounding Cherrie's disappearance.

In the wake of her vanishing, a meticulous and extensive search operation was launched, encompassing the rolling hills and dense woodlands surrounding her home. Bloodhounds, their senses keenly attuned to Cherrie's scent, scoured the terrain, accompanied by the persistent whir of helicopter blades overhead. Investigators, determined and methodical, conducted door-to-door inquiries, leaving no stone unturned in their quest for answers.

As news of Cherrie's disappearance spread, the community's response was immediate and heartening. Approximately 250 local volunteers, driven by a shared sense of urgency and compassion, joined the search efforts. They combed through the vast expanses of Butler County, their eyes scouring every inch of ground, hoping against hope to find Cherrie. In a remarkable display of solidarity, the local community raised a substantial sum of $39,000 as a reward for information leading to Cherrie's safe return. A local business, touched by the community's plight, added an additional $10,000 to the reward, specifically for information that would lead to the arrest and conviction of the person or persons responsible for her abduction.

Investigators, analyzing the situation with a critical eye, quickly ruled out the possibility of a ransom-driven kidnapping. Their focus shifted towards the likelihood that Cherrie might have known her abductor or abductors. However, in a relieving turn, all family members were swiftly cleared of any suspicion, their innocence affirmed through thorough investigation.

The case took a new turn with the emergence of a suspect vehicle – a bluish-green Dodge van with a distinctive mural. Public appeals for sightings of this unusual vehicle yielded crucial eyewitness accounts. Some reported seeing a van matching the description in New Kensington, heading towards Mount Pleasant. Intriguingly, other witnesses recalled seeing a blue car following the van. Adding to the mystery, there were claims that the van had been repainted black a week or two following Cherrie's disappearance, a move that suggested a conscious effort to evade detection.

As weeks turned into months with no significant breakthroughs, and with Cherrie missing for three months, the search for her took a national turn. A national direct mailing company took an unprecedented step in the search efforts. They printed postcards featuring Cherrie's photograph and an artist's rendition of the distinctive van. These postcards, poignant with the question "Have you seen me?" were distributed across thousands of households in the United States. They were slipped into telephone and utility bills, a silent appeal for help in a case that had captured the hearts of a nation.

Over the many years since Cherrie Ann Mahan vanished, the mystery of her disappearance has remained an enigma, a puzzle that investigators have tirelessly worked to solve. The Pennsylvania State Police and dedicated investigators have chased thousands of leads, hoping to uncover the truth about Cherrie's whereabouts and the identity of her abductor or abductors. These leads have spanned from potential sightings of Cherrie to the elusive vehicles spotted near the scene of her disappearance. Despite these efforts, Cherrie remains unfound, and the vehicles implicated in her abduction have never been located. The absence of concrete evidence has left open the haunting possibility that Cherrie might still be alive, a thought that both offers hope and deepens the mystery.

As the case has spanned decades, the Pennsylvania State Police have continued to receive tips and updates, a testament to the case's enduring impact and the community's refusal to let Cherrie's story be forgotten. In the year 2000, a renewed effort was made to find her. A computer-generated image depicting what Cherrie might look like at the age of 23 was circulated to thousands of households across America. Unfortunately, this initiative did not yield the breakthrough for which many had hoped.

In January 2011, a glimmer of hope emerged when Pennsylvania police received a tip described as potentially crucial. This tip, intriguingly, came from an individual who had known Cherrie. The specifics of this information were not publicly disclosed, with investigators citing the sensitivity and ongoing nature of the investigation. However, it was noted that this tip was more specific than any received in many years. Despite this, the police indicated that this new information suggested that Cherrie might no longer be alive.

Another significant moment in the investigation occurred in 2014. A tip suggested that Cherrie was alive, living under an assumed name in Michigan. This lead centered on a woman who had been adopted as a child and was uncertain of her origins. However, after DNA testing, it was confirmed that this woman was not Cherrie.

One of the most recent and chilling developments occurred in 2018. LeRoy McKinney, Cherrie's stepfather, received an anonymous handwritten letter. This letter hauntingly described who had murdered Cherrie, the reasons behind the act, and the location of her remains. The letter, ending with a hope for peace upon finding her body, added a somber and eerie dimension to the ongoing investigation.

Throughout these long years, Janice McKinney, Cherrie's mother, has remained steadfast in her belief that her daughter's disappearance can be solved. In 2020, Janice spoke of her conviction, revealing her belief that while Cherrie's biological father was not involved in the abduction, individuals associated with him might have been. She reflected on the circumstances surrounding Cherrie's conception, which she had claimed was a result of rape – a claim that had not been believed prior to Cherrie's disappearance. Poignantly, Janice shared that February 22, 1985, was the first day she had not been at the bottom of the driveway to meet her daughter after school, a deviation from routine that would forever haunt her.

The enduring mystery of Cherrie Ann Mahan's disappearance continues to resonate, a poignant reminder of the fragility of life and the relentless pursuit of truth by those left behind. The hope for closure, the quest for answers, and the resilience of a mother's love remain undiminished, even as the years pass by.